Language Stew

English is like language stew. English has words, spellings, and sounds from many different languages.

In this unit you will learn more about the words of the English language and how to recognize what they mean.

Building on Base Words

◢ Study It

How do words become part of our language? English words come from many languages. New words are added to name new things or new ideas. The word <u>Internet</u>, for example, has been a part of our language for only a short time. Sometimes English words are built from words we already have.

Look at these words.

Base Word	Word That Comes from the Base
electric	electricity
real	realistic

How can knowing a word's **base,** or origin, help you understand the word's meaning?

- You can use the base to help determine a word's meaning.
- You can recognize words that have similar base words.
- Knowing the base can help you remember a word's meaning.

Look at the second column in the chart. If you do not know what the word <u>electricity</u> means, you can see that it is similar to the word <u>electric</u>, a word that you do know. Can you think of other words that come from the base word <u>electric</u>?

Look at the last word in the first column. You may know that one meaning of the word <u>real</u> is "occurring in fact or something that is true." <u>Realistic</u> may be an unfamiliar word, but it has the same base as <u>real</u>, so you may reason that the meaning of realistic is "something that has the qualities of being true." Knowing the base word can give you an important clue to a word's meaning.

Word origins

◀ **Use It**

The following words come from base words. Write the base word for the underlined word in the blank.

 roll —————— 1. We rode the <u>roller</u> coaster.

phone —————— 2. The singer used a <u>microphone.</u>

Now you try it.

live —————— 1. The <u>lively</u> child danced across the floor.

Gym —————— 2. <u>Gymnastics</u> is a sport.

◀ **Practice It**

Look at the <u>underlined</u> word. Think about its base word. Circle the letter of the correct answer.

1. | The attic door made a <u>dreadful</u> creaking sound when she opened it.

   The base word for <u>dreadful</u> is *dread*. <u>Dreadful</u> means —

   A terrible

   B noisy

   C squeaky

   D loud

2. | The <u>government</u> will build a new highway around the city.

   The base word for <u>government</u> is *govern*. <u>Government</u> means —

   A rulers

   B truck drivers

   C cement suppliers

   D people

 Tip Look for the base word to help you understand a word's meaning.

Covering the Bases

Study It

Sometimes a word part is added to a base word. A **prefix** is added at the beginning of a word. A **suffix** is added at the end of a word. Prefixes and suffixes change the meanings of the base words.

Some examples of prefixes are *dis-*, meaning "not" or "away"; *pre-*, meaning "before"; and *un-*, meaning "not."

Some examples of suffixes are *-ful*, meaning "filled with"; *-less*, meaning "without"; and *-ment*, meaning "the state of."

If you know the meaning of the base word and the meaning of its prefix or suffix, you can determine what a word means.

Look at how these words were formed. Then look at their meanings.

Prefix or Suffix	Base Word	New Word
pre- means "before"	pay means "to give money for"	prepay means "to pay or give money for in advance"
-ful means "filled with"	hope means "to wish for and expect"	hopeful means "filled with hope"

What are the differences between the columns above?

- The first column has only word parts, or prefixes and suffixes.
- The second column has base words. Prefixes and suffixes can be added to base words to make new words.
- The third column includes the base word combined with the prefix or suffix to form a new word. The words in this column have meanings that combine the meaning of the base word and the meaning of its prefix or suffix.

Structural analysis

Look at this sentence. Think about the underlined word.

Jason tried to **disappear** after his last class of the day.

The base word underline{appear} means "to be in sight." The word underline{appear} has the prefix *dis-* added to it. The prefix *dis-* means "not," so underline{disappear} means "not to be in sight."

Look at this chart. Notice how the new words were formed.

Prefix or Suffix	Base Word	New Word
-less means "without"	life means "being alive"	lifeless means "without life"
-hood means "the condition of"	child means "a young person"	childhood means "the condition of being a young person"
-ly means "like"	friend means "one attached by affection"	friendly means "like one attached by affection"
-ist means "doer or believer"	art means "skill of creating"	artist means "one who does something very well" or "one who uses a skill to create"
-able means "can or able to"	trace means "to follow a path"	traceable means "able to be followed"
re- means "again"	new means "made fresh or made recently"	renew means "to make fresh again"
-er means "one who"	drive means "to operate a car"	driver means "one who drives"

Think about other words that combine base words with prefixes and suffixes. How would you figure out the meaning of these words?

- Look for the base word to see whether you know its meaning.
- Look for a prefix or a suffix and think about what it means.
- Combine the meaning of the base word with the meaning of the prefix or suffix to see whether the meaning of the new word makes sense in the sentence.

◢ Use It

Add a prefix or a suffix to the base word <u>underlined</u> in the sentence to make a word that fits in the sentence. Write the new word in the blank. Check the spelling of the new word.

_____quietly_____ 1. We <u>quiet</u> ly finished our homework.

_____teacher_____ 2. The <u>teach</u> er read to the students.

Now you try it.

___Sciencetist___ 1. The <u>science</u> ___ finished the experiment.

_____ ~~2.~~ Can you <u>ease</u> ___ complete your homework tonight?

_____ 3. The change in the weather was <u>notice</u> ___ when the wind blew harder.

_____ 4. John got in trouble for being ___ <u>honest</u>.

_____ 5. The ___ <u>finished</u> work needs to be completed.

_____ 6. The <u>organ</u> ___ played the song beautifully.

_____ 7. You need to ___ <u>try</u> that phone number if you did not get an answer.

_____ 8. Please ___ <u>place</u> the book when you are finished with it.

_____ 9. We put the <u>worth</u> ___ chair out with the trash.

_____ 10. We watched the <u>pitch</u> ___ throw the ball.

◢ Practice It

Read these sentences. Circle the letter of the correct answer.

1. | Mrs. Brown <u>rewound</u> the kite string. |

   The prefix *re-* in <u>rewound</u> means —

   A again

   B before

   C away

   D not

2. | The <u>shoeless</u> man waded into the water. |

   The suffix *-less* in <u>shoeless</u> means —

   A filled with

   B without

   C able to

   D condition of

3. | The <u>artist</u> painted several excellent pictures. |

   The suffix *-ist* in <u>artist</u> means —

   A like

   B filled with

   C one who does

   D condition of

4. | The <u>neighborhood</u> children played a game. |

   The suffix *-hood* in <u>neighborhood</u> means —

   A without

   B condition of being

   C doer or believer

   D like

 Look for base words, prefixes, and suffixes to understand unfamiliar words.

Find the Clues

◢ Study It

What can you do if you do not understand a word in a sentence? Sometimes you can use the words or sentences near the word to help you determine a word's meaning.

Look at this sentence. Notice the underlined word.

The students watched the play in the auditorium. They had seats near the stage.

What clues can help you find the meaning of auditorium?

- The sentence says that the students watched a play in the auditorium. So an auditorium must be a place, such as a room.

- The next sentence says that students had seats near the stage. Now you know that an auditorium has seats and a stage. So an auditorium must be a room with seats and a stage.

Look at this sentence. Notice the underlined word.

The airplane reached a high altitude.

The words airplane and high suggest the meaning of altitude, or the height at which the plane is flying.

What should you do when you read a word that you do not understand?

- Look at the words near the word to see what they suggest.

- Look at the other sentences near the word. Do they suggest what the word's meaning might be?

Context clues

Use It

In the sentences below, circle clue words that you can use to figure out the meaning of the underlined word. Then write the meaning for the underlined word in the blank. Look at the examples.

_____cold_____ 1. George put on a (sweater) because he was chilly.

_____surprised_____ 2. When Darcy walked up (behind) Matt, she startled him.

Now you try it.

_____ 1. The sun's reflection blinded Marie.

_____ 2. Mrs. Lee instructed several students.

Practice It

Look for clues about the meaning of the underlined word. Circle the letter of the correct answer.

1. After she ran three miles, Andrea was exhausted.

   A tired

   B placed

   C tiny

   D cool

2. The raven flew onto the tree branch and squawked.

   A mouse

   B bird

   C squirrel

   D cat

Tip Use words you know in a sentence to help you figure out the meaning of unfamiliar words.

More Than One Meaning

◢ Study It

This sentence might seem confusing at first. Lisa did Alex a favor when she brought the party favors. We know that <u>favor</u> is "a helpful act." <u>Favor</u> also can mean "an item used as a party gift."

Look at these words. Each word has more than one meaning.

Word	One Meaning	Second Meaning
loaf	to spend time lazily	a shaped mass of bread or meat
gorge	to eat greedily	a deep, narrow passage

- If a sentence is confusing, find any words in the sentence that may have more than one meaning.
- Reread the sentence, using another of the word's meanings.

Read this sentence. Think about the word <u>loaf</u>.

During my vacation, I plan to <u>loaf</u> for a whole day.

If you read the word <u>loaf</u> as "to spend time lazily," the sentence makes sense. If you use the other meaning of <u>loaf</u>, it does not.

Another way to find the correct meaning is to look at the word's part of speech. If the word is a noun, look for a meaning as a noun. If it is a verb, use an action meaning.

Read this sentence. Look at the word <u>gorge</u>.

They followed the <u>gorge</u> through the mountains.

"To eat greedily" does not make sense in the sentence because it expresses an action. "A deep narrow passage" does make sense because the word is used as a noun.

Multi-meaning words

Use It

Each word below has one meaning. Write another meaning for the word on the blank line.

a young student 1. pupil: a part of the eye that responds to light

a collection of information 2. file: a steel tool with a rough edge

Now you try it.

_____ 1. fast: to go without food

_____ 2. fleet: a group of ships

_____

Practice It

Choose the word that fits in both sentences. Circle the letter of the correct answer.

1. | We must _____ our own lunches for the field trip.
   We bought a table and chairs to _____ the dining room. |

   A furnish

   B make

   C buy

   D bring

2. | The school will _____ Jennifer to the art class.
   I will _____ that I am wrong when you show me proof. |

   A say

   B take

   C admit

   D confess

Tip
Choose the word that makes sense in the sentence.

Let's Find Out

◼ Study It

If you do not know the meaning of a word, you can look it up in a **dictionary.** A dictionary lists words in alphabetical order. If you want to learn synonyms or antonyms for a word, you can look the word up in a **thesaurus.**

Look at this entry from a dictionary.

The entry word is **ech • ō.** The dots break the word into syllables.

(ek´ō) The stress or accent marks between letters and the marks above letters show pronunciation.

ech • o (ek´ō) **n.** the repeating of a sound. plural, echoes. **v. 1.** to send back the sound of something **2.** to repeat or imitate closely

n. or **v.** These letters tell the word's part of speech.

Look at this entry from a thesaurus.

The entry word is **happy.**

adj. This abbreviation tells the word's part of speech.

happy **adj.** content, glad, joyful; antonym, sad

These words are synonyms.

This word is an antonym.

Resources

◢ Use It

Look at this example. Answer the questions.

_____echo_____ Write the entry word for the dictionary entry on page 12.

Now you try it.

_____ 1. How many syllables does <u>echo</u> have?

_____ 2. Write the plural of <u>echo</u> when it is used as a noun.

_____ 3. How many meanings does the verb <u>echo</u> have?

◢ Practice It

Read this dictionary entry. Circle the letter of the correct answer.

bi • cy • cle (bī′sik′əl) *n.* **1.** A vehicle made of a light frame on two wire-spoked wheels, one behind the other, and having a seat, handlebars for steering, brakes, and two pedals or a small motor by which it is driven. **2.** An exercise bicycle.

1. The entry word is —

   A bicycle

   B exercise

   C noun

   D vehicle

2. How many meanings does <u>bicycle</u> have?

   A one

   B two

   C three

   D four

 For a dictionary test question, look at each part of the entry to find the answer.

Unit 1
Test-Taking Strategy

Strategy: Find Clues

In this unit you learned how to take a closer look at words. You discovered that you can learn the meaning of an unfamiliar word by looking at the words and sentences around the word. Looking for clues outside the word can help you answer questions about the meaning of a word.

- Read the sentence. Can you guess the meaning of the underlined word? Use the words around it as clues. Also look for clues in the sentences before and after the word.

- Compare your answer to each answer choice. Which is the closest match?

Try It Out

Choose the word that means about the same as the <u>underlined</u> word. Fill in the circle next to the correct answer.

> Marie drove with her dad to the train station to wait for a parcel. When the train arrived, Marie watched with excitement. Porters unloaded suitcases and freight packages. There it was! Her father signed for the parcel. Then they both picked up the box and carried it out to the car.

In this paragraph the word <u>parcel</u> means —

A a suitcase

B a train station

C a package

D a car

Marie and her father wait for the parcel to arrive by train. The words <u>porters</u> and <u>unloaded</u> tell you that people took things out of the train. Marie and her father lift the box and carry it to their car. A parcel is a package of some kind. So, the correct answer is **C.**

Unit 1 • Vocabulary
Put It to the Test

This test will check what you have learned in this unit.

DIRECTIONS: Circle the letter of the correct answer.

1. | Hannah has just learned to swim. She practices in the <u>shallow</u> end of the pool. |

   The opposite of <u>shallow</u> is —

   A narrow

   B deep

   C full

   D low

2. | You may need a <u>wrench</u> to do bike repairs. |

   The word <u>wrench</u> means a type of —

   A book

   B tool

   C light

   D box

3. | Turn down that _____ coming from the radio.

   Hold your _____ like this to hit the ball. |

   The word that fits both sentences is —

   A noise

   B bat

   C music

   D racket

4. | Our host was at the front door to <u>greet</u> all the guests. |

   The word <u>greet</u> means —

   A address

   B welcome

   C hear

   D search

5. | Who won the 30-yard _____ ?

   Sprinkle a _____ of salt on your popcorn. |

   The word that fits both sentences is —

   A teaspoon

   B race

   C dash

   D handful

6. | The cat eyed the dog <u>cautiously</u>. |

   The word <u>cautiously</u> means —

   A quickly

   B happily

   C peacefully

   D carefully

GO ON

Achieve It! Practice Cards

_____

7. The gardener whistled a <u>cheerful</u> tune as she mowed the grass.

The base word for <u>cheerful</u> is *cheer*. <u>Cheerful</u> means —

A full of joy

B full of confusion

C full of anger

D full of sadness

8. Rita divided the pizza <u>equally</u> among 16 guests.

The ending *-ly* in the word <u>equally</u> is called a —

A simile

B prefix

C suffix

D base word

9. There was an <u>uneasy</u> quiet in the room after Todd broke the picture.

The prefix *un-* means —

A not

B on

C in

D very

pres • i • dent (prez´i dənt) *n.* the chief officer of a country, a company, a club, or another organization

10. What part of speech is the word <u>president</u>?

A adjective

B verb

C noun

D adverb

11. Which syllable in <u>president</u> is pronounced the most strongly?

A first

B second

C third

D all are equal

Achieve It! Practice Cards

_____

Understanding What You Read

Open the Door!

Sometimes you open a door to a place you've never been before. When you get inside, you need to find your way around. Opening a book is like opening a door. You enter a place where you can learn something new or find something to enjoy. First, you need to be sure you can "find your way around" as you read.

In this unit you will learn skills to help you find your way around, or understand, what you read.

Prove It!

◣ Study It

A **fact** is a statement or sentence that you can prove. You can look up a fact in a book. You can prove facts by using your senses: sight, hearing, touch, taste, and smell. Different people agree that the same facts are true. The sentence *Bicycles have two wheels* is a fact that can be proved. You can look at a bicycle and see that it has two wheels.

An **opinion** is a sentence or statement that tells a belief or feeling. You cannot prove an opinion. Different people have different opinions. The sentence *Kittens are the best pets* is an opinion because some people might think dogs or birds are the best pets.

Sometimes there are clues that help you find an opinion. Words like best, worst, should, feel, think, and believe can tell you that a sentence is an opinion.

Read this chart. It shows examples of facts and opinions.

Sentence	Can It Be Proved?	Fact or Opinion?
A banana is a fruit.	Yes	Fact
I think red is the prettiest color.	No	Opinion
John Glenn was the first U.S. astronaut to orbit the earth.	Yes	Fact
Bears should live in the zoo.	No	Opinion
George Washington was the first president of the United States.	Yes	Fact
I believe that our school band is the best in the state.	No	Opinion

Fact/opinion

Use It

In the blanks before each sentence, write the word <u>fact</u> or <u>opinion</u>. Look at these examples.

1. _____opinion_____ Dogs are wonderful pets.

2. _____fact_____ Texas is part of the United States.

Now you try it.

1. _____ I think oranges are delicious.

2. _____ Mr. Riley is the best teacher in the school.

3. _____ Polar bears are white.

4. _____ Pine trees grow in North America.

Practice It

Read each question. Circle the letter of the correct answer.

1. **Which sentence is a FACT?**

   A People should ride bikes more often.

   B Abraham Lincoln was a United States president.

   C Our team has the best players.

   D That movie was awful.

2. **Which sentence is an OPINION?**

   A Bears eat meat and plants.

   B Sacramento is the capital of California.

   C I think we should go swimming today.

   D The law in our state says that you must wear a seatbelt.

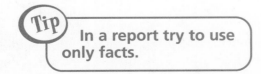

Tip In a report try to use only facts.

Same but Different

◣ Study It

Think about your brother or sister or your friend. How are you and that person alike? To answer this question, you need to **compare** yourself to that person.

How are you and your brother, sister, or friend different? To answer this question, you need to **contrast** yourself with that person.

When you compare, you look for ways that things are alike. When you contrast, you look for ways that things are different.

When you compare, you might use these words.

<u>alike</u>   <u>same</u>   <u>both</u>   <u>as</u>   <u>just as</u>   <u>similar to</u>

When you contrast, you might use these words.

<u>different</u>   <u>but</u>   <u>however</u>   <u>in contrast</u>   <u>unlike</u>

Read the passage below. Look at the <u>underlined</u> words that show comparison and contrast.

> <u>Both</u> my brother and I love to ride our bikes. We have the <u>same</u> kind of bike, <u>but</u> my brother's bike has a bell. When we ride our bikes, it is hard to tell us apart because we look a lot <u>alike</u>. We <u>both</u> have red hair and green eyes, <u>but</u> our haircuts are <u>different</u>, and my brother is the one ringing the bell on his bike!

In the passage above, the author uses the words <u>both</u>, <u>same</u>, and <u>alike</u> to compare. The words <u>different</u> and <u>but</u> show contrast.

Sometimes an author compares and contrasts things in the same paragraph, as the author did above. At other times, an author may compare in one paragraph and contrast in the next paragraph.

Compare and contrast

Read the passage. Look at the underlined words that compare and contrast.

      Rabbits and hares are <u>alike</u> in many ways. <u>Both</u> have long ears, big eyes, and short, fluffy tails. <u>Both</u> rabbits and hares have excellent hearing and can run very fast.

      In other ways they are <u>different</u>. Hares live alone in open fields. <u>However</u>, rabbits like to live in groups. Rabbits are usually smaller than hares.

In the passage above, the author compares the two animals in the first paragraph and contrasts them in the second paragraph

rabbit

Look at the Venn diagram below. It shows how you can compare and contrast hares and rabbits.

Hares	**Both**	**Rabbits**
Live alone	Long ears	Live in groups
Larger than rabbits	Big eyes	Smaller than hares
Live in open fields	Short, fluffy tails	
	Good hearing	
	Fast runners	

Using a Venn diagram can help you understand how things are alike and how they are different.

hare

Read the passage. Underline the words that tell you that things are being compared or contrasted.

Today you can watch movies on television, or you can see them in a movie theater. You can often see the same movie in both places. You can even eat popcorn in both places. But watching a movie at the theater is different from watching it on television. The theater has a bigger screen, and the sound is better than it is on a television set at home. You may see scenes from upcoming movies, or previews, in a theater. Television movies are usually interrupted for commercials, but movies at a movie theater are not. Finally, there are usually more people watching the movie in the theater.

Read the Venn diagram below. Then fill in the blanks.

Television
Small screen

_____

_____

Both
Show same movie

_____

Movie Theater
Bigger screen

_____

Previews

_____

Practice It

Read this passage. Then read the questions. Circle the letter of the correct answer.

Snowboarding and skiing are both popular winter sports. These sports are alike in many ways. Find a snowy mountain, and you will find skiers and snowboarders. Skiers and snowboarders use many of the same movements as they swish down a mountain.

Unlike skiers, snowboarders use one board strapped to both of their feet. Skiers have two boards, one strapped to each foot. Skiers also use poles to help them balance. But snowboarders balance without help and even do tricks with their boards. Although snow skiing has been around for a long time, more people every year are taking up snowboarding.

1. **How are snowboarding and skiing ALIKE?**

   A Both sports use poles.

   B Both sports take place in snow.

   C Both sports use one board.

   D Both sports use two boards.

2. **How are snowboarders DIFFERENT from skiers?**

   A Snowboarders need snow.

   B Snowboarders use poles.

   C Snowboarders use mountain runs.

   D Snowboarders use one board.

3. **Which statement about the passage is TRUE?**

   A The first paragraph tells how the sports are different.

   B The second paragraph tells how the sports are different.

   C The first paragraph is only about skiing.

   D The second paragraph is only about snowboarding.

 Tip Remember that comparing shows how things are alike and contrasting shows how they are different.

What Happened and Why?

■ Study It

One way writers explain something is by using **cause** and **effect** sentences. You can find a cause and an effect by asking the right questions and looking for signal words.

Cause	Effect
Ask, *Why did it happen?*	Ask, *What happened?*
A **cause** tells <u>why</u> something happened.	An **effect** explains <u>what</u> happened.

Look for word clues in a passage to find causes and effects. Signal words such as <u>because</u>, <u>since</u>, <u>after</u>, <u>before</u>, and <u>as a result</u> are often used in cause and effect sentences.

Writers sometimes tell you about an effect before they tell you the cause. You will need to ask the right questions and look for signal words to find the cause and the effect.

Read this sentence. Then look at the chart.

> Turtles come out of their winter homes when the weather gets warm.

Cause (Why Did It Happen?)	Effect (What Happened?)
The weather gets warm.	Turtles come out of their winter homes.

In this sentence the cause is the warm weather. The effect is that turtles come out of their winter homes.

When you look for cause and effect, remember the following.

- Cause and effect help readers answer the questions <u>why</u> and <u>what</u>.
- Cause and effect can usually be found by looking for signal words.

Cause and effect

Sometimes a paragraph can have more than one cause and effect. In some paragraphs you may find two causes and two effects. In other paragraphs you may find several effects from one cause.

Read this passage. Look for more than one cause and effect.

The Final Baseball Game

The Hampton Hawks were finally playing in the championship game, but the score was tied. Then Joe Malik came up to bat for the Hawks. On the first pitch, he swung hard and hit a home run. The tie was broken! As a result the Hawks became the league champions.

Look at the chart that shows the causes and effects in the passage.

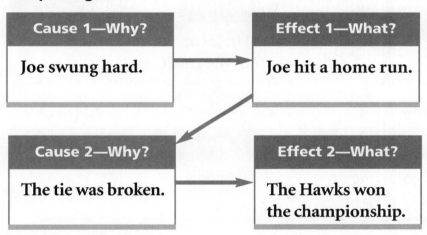

Cause 1—Why?	Effect 1—What?
Joe swung hard.	Joe hit a home run.

Cause 2—Why?	Effect 2—What?
The tie was broken.	The Hawks won the championship.

You can use a chart like this one to help you find more than one cause and effect in a passage. Remember to ask *Why did something happen?* and *What happened?* when you read.

Read this passage. Look for causes and effects. Underline the signal words that show cause and effect.

The Strange Effect

Dr. Jacobs was in her secret lab working on a special project. She quickly threw a jar into the trash because slime started to ooze from it. The slime had already covered her hands. As a result, her hands began to glow. After she got home, her family said she looked like a space alien.

Look at the chart. Fill in the empty box in each chart.

Cause (Why Did It Happen?)	Effect (What Happened?)
Slime oozed from a jar.	Dr. Jacobs threw the jar in the trash.

Now you try it.

Cause (Why Did It Happen?)	Effect (What Happened?)
Dr. Jacobs got slime on her hands.	

Cause (Why Did It Happen?)	Effect (What Happened?)
Dr. Jacobs's hands were glowing.	

Practice It

Read this passage from *Duck* by Barrie Watts. Look for causes and effects. Then read the questions. Circle the letter of the correct answer.

It takes up to 48 hours for the duckling to break out of the egg completely. It is tired and its feathers are wet. The duckling's mother keeps it warm until its feathers dry out. The duckling still has some of the egg yolk in its body. Over the next few days it will use the yolk for food, until it is strong enough to find something to eat.

1. **What causes the duckling to be tired and wet?**

   A Its mother keeps it warm.

   B It uses the yolk for food.

   C It has just broken out of its egg.

   D It has just learned to swim.

2. **Why does a duckling need to use some of the yolk for food?**

   A Its mother does not have any food.

   B It is not strong enough to find its own food.

   C Ducklings never eat other kinds of food.

   D The mother does not want it to waste food.

3. **How does the duckling stay warm?**

   A The yolk makes it warm.

   B It is warm because it gets stronger.

   C The mother keeps it warm.

   D It is warm in the egg.

Tip When you read, use cause and effect charts to help you understand why things happen.

Big Picture

◢ Study It

Most paragraphs in a nonfiction passage have a **main idea.** The main idea tells you who or what the paragraph is mostly about. **Detail** sentences in each paragraph support the main idea.

When you read, look for the main idea. Then ask yourself how each detail in the paragraph supports the main idea.

- Each paragraph has a main idea.
- Each sentence in a paragraph contains details that support the main idea.

Details can

- explain a main idea
- answer important questions, such as <u>where</u>, <u>when</u>, <u>why</u>, and <u>how</u>
- give facts, examples, and reasons that support the main idea

Read this paragraph. Think about the main idea and details. Then look at the chart.

Chimpanzees are very friendly animals. They enjoy being together. When chimpanzees meet, they greet each other with pats on the back and holding hands. They may part and comb each other's hair. Chimpanzees like quiet, friendly physical contact with one another.

Main Idea
Chimpanzees are friendly animals that like physical contact.

Detail	Detail	Detail
They enjoy being together.	They greet each other with back pats and by holding hands.	They part and comb each other's hair.

Main idea/supporting details

Read this paragraph. Think about the main idea and details. Then look at the chart.

Roald Dahl became interested in writing books for children when he made up bedtime stories for his own children. Some of Roald Dahl's best-known books are *James and the Giant Peach* and *Charlie and the Chocolate Factory*. His books are found in many libraries and bookstores. Roald Dahl is one of today's most popular children's writers.

Main Idea
Roald Dahl is one of today's most popular children's writers.

Detail	Detail	Detail
He has written many well-known books.	**His books are found in libraries and bookstores.**	**Dahl's books include *James and the Giant Peach* and *Charlie and the Chocolate Factory*.**

Remember, the main idea is who or what the paragraph is about. The detail sentences tell <u>when</u>, <u>where</u>, <u>why</u>, and <u>how</u> something happens.

Read this passage. The main idea is circled. Underline each detail. Then write the details in the chart.

⟨Icebergs come in different shapes and sizes.⟩ One iceberg may be domed, with a rounded top like that of an old mountain. Another may be blocky, a big square slab of floating ice. Some icebergs are small, but others are several miles long. In 1996 an iceberg larger than the state of Rhode Island broke away from Antarctica. When you see an iceberg, you only see part of it. The part above water is just the tip. The part you do not see is many times bigger than the tip.

Main Idea
Icebergs come in different shapes and sizes.

Detail	Detail	Detail	Detail
		Some are small, but others are several miles long.	

Practice It

Read the passage and look at the chart. Then read the question. Circle the letter of the correct answer.

Cats have many ways to communicate, or share information, with each other. Sometimes they use their bodies, and sometimes they make sounds. One way that cats let other cats know that they are angry or afraid is to make faces. Cats also move their tails to communicate. They may hold their tails straight up to say, "I feel friendly." If they are unhappy, they may move their tails back and forth. Cats make sounds like meowing, hissing, or growling. Some sounds can mean "hello," while other sounds can mean "leave me alone."

Main Idea
Cats have many ways to communicate with each other.

Detail	Detail	Detail
	Cats use their bodies to communicate.	Cats make sounds to communicate.

1. **Which is the BEST detail to fill in the empty box?**

   A Cats hunt and catch birds.

   B Cats chase one another.

   C Cats make faces to communicate.

   D Cats communicate.

Tip To find the main idea, ask yourself who or what the paragraph is MOSTLY about.

In Other Words

Study It

When you read, it is a good idea to put the author's ideas into your own words. Using your own words helps you understand the information and remember what you have read.

There are two ways to put ideas into your own words. You can write a **summary,** or you can **paraphrase** a passage.

When you write a summary, write down only the main ideas and most important details of a passage. A summary is shorter than the original passage.

To write a summary, you should

- look for main ideas and important details
- write in your own words
- be sure that the information is correct and written clearly

Read this passage. Then look at the chart.

In the early 1600s, people came from England to North America. In North America they set up colonies. These colonists wanted a new life. North America was a beautiful and mostly unexplored continent. Many people dreamed of owning their own land there. In England some colonists had not owned their own land. Some people also came to America so that they could be free to practice their religion.

Summary Chart	
Main Idea: The colonists wanted a new life.	**Summary:**
Detail: came to North America from England **Detail:** came in early 1600s **Detail:** wanted to own land **Detail:** wanted to practice their own religion	Colonists came to North America from England in the early 1600s. They came so they could own land and have religious freedom.

Paraphrase/summarize

Paraphrasing can help you understand difficult passages. When you paraphrase, you are rewriting a passage without changing its meaning.

When you paraphrase, look up difficult words and replace them with synonyms. You can also put the words in a different order. Finally, make sure the paraphrase is about the same length as the original passage.

A paraphrase is useful for taking notes for a report, but you would not paraphrase a whole book.

Read this passage.

> "My country 'tis of thee,
> Sweet land of liberty,
> Of thee I sing.
> Land where my fathers died!
> Land of the Pilgrim's pride!
> From every mountain side,
> Let freedom ring!"

Use a dictionary to look up words that you do not understand.

father means "forefather or ancestor"

liberty means "freedom from control"

Pilgrim means "any of the group of English Puritans who founded Plymouth Colony in 1620"

'tis is a contraction of it is

Now read this paraphrase of the passage above.

> I am singing about my country, a land of freedom.
> My ancestors died here.
> The Pilgrims were proud of this land.
> Let the sound of freedom ring out from every mountain.

Read the passage. Underline any difficult words. Then write the answers to the questions.

(1) Corals are saltwater animals. (2) They grow where the ocean is shallow and temperate. (3) After many years the little corals build huge reefs. (4) A coral reef is similar to a vibrant, submerged garden.

(5) Plants and animals live in the coral reef. (6) The reef has many holes where animals can live. (7) Lobsters and octopuses can live in a coral reef. (8) Brightly colored sponges grow on the rocks. (9) Snails, sea stars, and many fish come to the reef to consume the sponges. (10) Butterfly fish and grouper are just a few of the kinds of fish found there.

1. **How would you paraphrase sentence 2?**

   _____

   _____

2. **How would you paraphrase sentence 4?**

   _____

   _____

3. **How would you paraphrase sentence 9?**

   _____

   _____

Practice It

Read the passage and look at the chart. Then read the questions. Circle the letter of the correct answer.

(1) Native Americans in the Pacific Northwest used to make totem poles. (2) Each totem pole told a story. (3) The decorative poles were enhanced with animals and faces. (4) Some were painted. (5) Totem poles passed on family histories and legends and marked the places where families lived. (6) The totem poles were often placed along riverbanks so that people in canoes could see them.

Summary Chart	
Main Idea:	**Summary:**
Detail: told stories **Detail:** told family histories and legends **Detail:** marked where a family lived	Native Americans in the Pacific Northwest used totem poles to record stories, legends, and family histories. A totem pole also marked where a family lived.

1. **What main idea should be placed in the chart?**

   A Totem poles had animals and faces carved on them.

   B Native Americans lived in the Pacific Northwest.

   C Native Americans had family villages.

   D Native Americans in the Pacific Northwest used to make totem poles.

2. **Which sentence is the best paraphrase of sentence 3?**

   A The poles were made out of animals.

   B Animals made the poles with pictures of faces.

   C The poles had animals and faces carved on them.

   D Animals used their faces to make the poles.

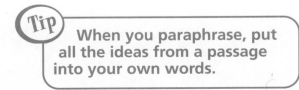

Tip When you paraphrase, put all the ideas from a passage into your own words.

Lesson 11

What's the Point?

◢ Study It

An author always has a **purpose,** or reason, for writing. Usually the author does not tell you directly what the purpose is. Instead, you need to look for hints.

Look at the chart. It shows different reasons why authors write.

Author's Purpose
to persuade, or get you to agree with an idea or to do something
to express feelings
to entertain
to inform or tell about something

When you read something, ask yourself some questions.

- Who is the audience?
- What kind of writing is it? Is it a poem? Is it a story? Is it an article? Is it a play? Is it journal writing?
- What is the topic or subject?

Then ask yourself these questions to learn the author's purpose.

- Does the writing mostly show personal feelings?
- Does the writing try to entertain the reader?
- Does the writing give information or explain something?
- Does the writing try to get me to agree with an idea?

Author's purpose

Read the letter. Suppose that Goldilocks is a real person and that she wrote this letter after she visited the house of the three bears. Think about her purpose.

Dear Mother,

You should feel sorry for me. I was hungry after skipping through the woods. Then I saw a house with the door wide open, and there was soup on the table. It smelled delicious. I didn't want the soup to get cold, so I ate it.

After I ate, I was sleepy. So I climbed into the smallest bed and fell asleep.

When the owners came home, they screamed at me. I was really afraid. I jumped up and ran home. I didn't do anything wrong.

Love,
Goldilocks

Who is the audience?	Goldilocks is writing to her mother.
What kind of writing is it?	It is a letter.
What is the writing about?	Goldilocks's visit to the house of the three bears.
What is the purpose of the letter?	Goldilocks wants to persuade her mother that she did not do anything wrong.

Goldilocks wrote the letter to persuade her mother.

She did not write to entertain her mother. If that had been her purpose, she would have written a different letter. She might have told how funny things were.

She did not write to give information about the three bears' house. A letter with that purpose would have told what all the rooms were like and what the food tasted like.

She did not write just to say how afraid she was either. If that were her purpose, she probably would have written a lot about her feelings.

Read this passage. Look for hints about the author's purpose. Then answer the question.

It is important to wear a helmet while riding a bicycle. There are as many as 45,000 head injuries to children each year. The laws of many states say that anyone under the age of sixteen who rides a bike must wear a helmet. But some states still do not have a helmet law. All states need to have laws about bike helmets. It would make bicycling safer for all children.

What is the author's purpose?
to persuade

Now you try it.

Read this poem. Then read the question. Write your answer on the line.

The Library

I choose a book and on its pages
I enter a world of knights and sages.
The dragon is winning—no, now the knight!
I think I know who'll win this fight.
In another book we're making bread
the same way as my Uncle Ted!
(Let it rise, push it down,
bake until the top is brown.)
Now I follow one small bear
through the forest, to his favorite chair.
There are so many worlds inside these books
no matter on which shelf I look.

1. What is the author's purpose?

_____

Practice It

Read this letter. Then read the items. Circle the letter of the correct answer.

> Dear City Planner,
>
> I am a fourth-grade student at Valley Park School. I have been worried about all of the traffic around our school. Every day I see more and more cars. I walk to school, and it takes a long time to cross the street with so much traffic. I think it would be a good idea to put a crossing guard on the corner near my school. Then I will be able to cross the street more safely. Please talk about it at your next meeting.
>
> James Graffin

1. **The main purpose of the letter is to —**

   A persuade

   B entertain

   C give facts

   D tell a story

2. **What does the writer of the letter want the city planner to do?**

   A tell fourth graders not to worry

   B solve the traffic problems

   C provide a school crossing guard

   D visit the school

3. **The writer tries to achieve his purpose by —**

   A ordering the city planner to act

   B talking about what a good student he is

   C telling about his own experiences

   D offering to serve as a crossing guard

Tip As you read, think about the writer's purpose.

Lesson 12

Picture This!

◢ Study It

Graphics are **charts, maps, diagrams, graphs,** or **pictures** that show information. Writers sometimes use graphics when there are too many facts and numbers to include in a paragraph. Graphics arrange information so that it is easy to understand.

Graphics show information in different ways.

- Charts put information in a certain order.
- Maps show where places are.
- Diagrams show steps for doing something, how parts of things fit together, or how a process works.
- Graphs compare information.
- Pictures can be drawings or photographs. They show what something looks like.

Here are some helpful hints for understanding graphics.

- Read the title. It tells you the topic of the graphic.
- Read the labels on the side and the bottom of graphs. These labels tell you what each bar, mark, or figure means.
- Read all the words. They will tell you more about the graphic.
- If you are looking at a map, look at the map key to understand what the symbols, or marks, mean.
- Look at all the numbers if there are any. Are they percents? Are they dollars? Are they in tens or hundreds?
- Look at the highest, or greatest, number if the chart or graph has numbers. Then look for the lowest, or least, number.

Graphics

Look at this chart.

	Pages Read by Students During the Week					
Student	**Days of the Week**					
	Mon.	**Tue.**	**Wed.**	**Thurs.**	**Fri.**	**Total**
Catherine	6	7	0	0	1	14
Kaya	0	2	1	2	2	7
Raymond	3	2	1	0	3	9
Raphael	0	2	1	1	0	4

Here is what this chart tells you.

- The title tells you that the chart is about the number of pages read by students during a week.

- The labels for each column tell you what kind of information is in each column. For example, the first column lists students' names, and the next five columns list the days of the week. The last column lists the total number of pages read by each student for the week.

- The rows tell you how many pages each student read each day and the total number of pages that each student read in five days.

Now you can answer these questions.

Which student read the most pages during the week?	Catherine
Which student read the fewest pages during the week?	Raphael
Who did not read any pages on Friday?	Raphael
How many pages did Kaya read in the week?	7 pages
What is the title of the chart?	"Pages Read by Students During the Week"

◣ Use It

Look at this chart. Then answer the questions.

Average High and Low Temperatures in June		
City	**High**	**Low**
Anchorage	62°	47°
Denver	81°	52°
New York	79°	63°
Phoenix	104°	73°
Pittsburgh	79°	57°
Seattle	70°	52°

Look at these examples.

1. What is the title of the chart?
   Average High and Low Temperatures in June

2. Which city has the lowest average temperature in June?
   Anchorage

Now you try it.

1. What cities are listed on the chart?

   _____

   _____

2. Which city has the highest average temperature?

   _____

3. Which city has a high average temperature of 81°?

   _____

4. Which city has a low average temperature of 57°?

   _____

◢ Practice It

A **circle graph** is another kind of graphic. It is sometimes called a **pie chart** because each part of the circle looks like a slice of pie.

Look at the circle graph. Then read the items. Circle the letter of the correct answer.

Daily Activities

Sleep 9 hours
School 6 hours
Playing 4 hours
Eating 3 hours
Homework 2 hours

1. **What activity takes up the MOST amount of time in a day?**

   A sleeping

   B playing

   C eating

   D school

2. **This circle graph tells you that —**

   A doing homework takes up more time than sleeping

   B most of a day is spent eating

   C more time is spent at school than playing

   D eating takes up less time than doing homework

3. **Which activity takes up the LEAST amount of time in a day?**

   A eating

   B homework

   C school

   D playing

Tip Read the titles and labels carefully when you look at a graphic.

Unit 2
Test-Taking Strategy

Strategy: Find the Main Idea

In this unit you learned that paragraphs and passages have a main idea that is supported by detail sentences. The main idea is what the paragraph is mostly about. Sometimes it is not stated directly.

Use this strategy to help you find the main idea of a paragraph.

- Read the entire paragraph. Ask yourself, *Who or what is this paragraph mostly about?* Circle any sentences that answer this question.

- Then look for details that support the main idea. Remember to ask <u>when</u>, <u>where</u>, <u>how</u>, and <u>why</u> to find the details. Underline sentences that answer these questions.

Try It Out

Read this passage. Then read the question. Circle the letter of the correct answer.

> Earth has seasons because it is tilted. In July the Northern Hemisphere is tilted toward the sun. That makes it summer in the United States. Six months later Earth has circled half way around the sun. The Northern Hemisphere then tilts away from the sun. That makes it winter in the United States.

What is the main idea of this passage?

A   Earth has seasons because it is tilted.

B   Winter is cold in the United States.

C   Summer is hot in the United States.

D   The United States is in the Northern Hemisphere.

The main idea is stated in the first sentence. The rest of the paragraph gives you details about how seasons happen. **A** is the correct answer.

Unit 2 • Understanding What You Read
Put It to the Test

This test will check what you have learned in this unit.

DIRECTIONS: Read the passage. Then read each item. Circle the letter of the correct answer.

Spaceship Earth

1 Even as you are sitting still, Earth is moving. You can't feel it, but Earth travels in two different ways. It spins around like a top. At the same time, Earth moves around the sun. The way Earth spins is unlike the way it moves around the sun. It is amazing that Earth does both of these things at once.

2 How does Earth's spinning cause day and night? Day changes into night and back again because Earth spins. When sunlight shines on part of Earth, it is daytime there. As that part of Earth moves away from the sun, that part gets darker. Finally, when that part of Earth is no longer getting any sunlight, it is nighttime there. On one side of the planet, it is daytime, while on the opposite side it is night. Each day is 24 hours long because that is how long it takes for Earth to spin around completely.

1. **Which of these sentences is an OPINION from the passage?**

   A A day is 24 hours long.

   B Earth moves around the sun.

   C Sunlight causes daytime.

   D It is amazing that Earth does both of these things at once.

GO ON

Achieve It! Practice Cards

_____

2. **Which statement is a FACT from the passage?**

   A You cannot see the moon from Earth.

   B It takes 24 hours for Earth to spin around completely.

   C Earth spins around the moon.

   D You can feel Earth spinning.

3. **In this passage Earth is compared to —**

   A a top

   B the moon

   C the sun

   D a light

4. **The main purpose of this passage is to —**

   A entertain

   B persuade

   C inform or explain

   D express feelings

5. **What is paragraph 2 MOSTLY about?**

   A how Earth's spinning causes day and night

   B how many hours there are in a day

   C when it is daytime in the United States

   D how Earth moves around the sun

6. | The way Earth spins is unlike the way it moves around the sun. |
   |---|

   What key word in this sentence does the author use to show contrast?

   A moves

   B around

   C unlike

   D spins

7. | Earth spins. That is why we have day and night. A day is 24 hours long. It takes 24 hours for Earth to spin around completely. |
   |---|

   Which of these sentences could you add to this summary of paragraph 2?

   A Earth spins like a top.

   B Even as you are sitting still, Earth is moving.

   C It is amazing that Earth does both of these things at once.

   D As one part of Earth spins away from the sun, day changes into night there.

GO ON

Achieve It! Practice Cards

8.

> I think students should have a say in the design of this new school playground. If you vote for me for class president, I will make sure that your ideas are heard.

In the passage above, the author's purpose is —

A to entertain

B to persuade

C to tell information

D to express feelings

9. When an author writes about a cause and effect, he or she is telling you —

A why you should agree with his or her opinion

B why something happened and what happened

C how two things are the same and different

D how to make something

10. When you write a summary, you should —

A write the main ideas and details of a passage in your own words

B include the author's name

C include every detail in the passage

D write the same number of words as the passage

11. A FACT is —

A what someone thinks

B something that can be proved to be true

C a belief about something

D not always true

12. What should you do when you paraphrase?

A copy every word from the passage

B read the passage out loud

C skip over the hard words in the passage

D look up hard words and rewrite the passage in your own words

13. The details in a passage give facts about —

A the introduction

B the title

C the conclusion

D the main idea

GO ON

Achieve It! Practice Cards

Look at the chart. Circle the letter of the correct answer.

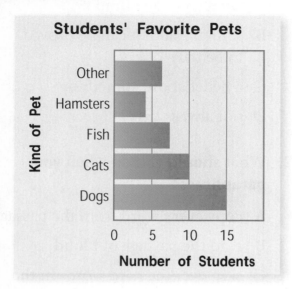

14. **The graph shows that these students —**

    A like fish more than cats

    B like fish more than dogs

    C like cats more than fish

    D like hamsters more than fish

15. **The graph shows that —**

    A most students do not like pets

    B students like hamsters the most

    C students like fish and cats the same

    D dogs are the most popular pet

16. **How many students said that cats were their favorite pet?**

    A 10

    B 15

    C 8

    D 6

Look at the chart. Circle the letter of the correct answer.

Student	Score on First Test	Score on Second Test
Marla	96	100
Scott	76	97
Isa	87	35
Kim	68	69

17. **This chart shows —**

    A which student did best on the homework

    B which student did best on the first test

    C which student is oldest

    D which student is new in the class

STOP

Achieve It! Practice Cards

Connect the Details!

When you build a project with Legos®, you need all of the correct pieces to finish it. When all the pieces are snapped together, the project is strong and complete. Reading a book is like this, too.

In this unit you will learn to connect facts and details to get the complete message in a reading passage.

Using Clues

◾ Study It

As a student you often read to learn new information. You learn new things directly from the facts and details in a passage. However, you can often learn new information even when it is "hidden," or not directly written in a passage. The facts and details in a passage are like clues. You use these clues and what you already know to find hidden information. This is called making an **inference.** The inference is the hidden information you find.

Read this sentence. Pay attention to the underlined words.

John <u>looked at the clock</u> and <u>ran out of the house.</u>

Use this chart to make an inference.

Question: What inference can I make about John from this sentence?

Clues from Sentence		What I Know		Inference
• John looked at the clock. • John ran out of the house.		• Clocks show the time. • People run when they are in a hurry.		• John is late and needs to get somewhere in a hurry.

First, read the clues from the sentence. The sentence says that John looked at the clock and then ran out of the house.

Then, add what you know to the clues from the sentence. You know that

- clocks show the time
- people run when they are in a hurry

The clues from the sentence plus what you already know help you make the inference that John is late and needs to get somewhere in a hurry.

Make inferences

Inferences are ideas that are based on the passage but do not actually appear in the passage. Inferences can help you figure out

- the main idea of a passage
- what characters in a story think or feel
- the reason why something happened

Read this passage. Some clues are <u>underlined</u>.

Subways are underground trains in big cities. Boston and New York have subways. <u>Subways move many people very quickly.</u> They are <u>crowded between 7:00 A.M. and 9:00 A.M.</u> They are also <u>crowded from 4:00 P.M. to 6:30 P.M.</u>

Now look at this chart. It shows an inference you can make from the clues and what you already know.

Question: What inference can I make about subways from this passage?		
Clues from Passage • Subways move people quickly. • Subways are crowded at certain hours.	**What I Know** • People travel between home and school or work at these times.	**Inference** • People use subways to get to work and school.

Use It

Read this passage from *The Mystery in San Francisco* by Gertrude Chandler Warner. Underline clues about what the Alden family is doing.

First thing in the morning, Aunt Jane said, "Andy, here's your cap." She handed him the baseball cap containing the four slips of paper.

"Hurry, Uncle Andy!" Benny said.

The Aldens watched as Uncle Andy reached into the hat. He drew out a piece of paper and looked at it.

"What does it say?" Violet asked.

Uncle Andy smiled. "I think I'll keep it a surprise," he said, and put the paper in his pocket.

At first the Aldens were disappointed. They didn't want to wait another minute to find out where they were going.

Then Jessie said, "That's a good idea, Uncle Andy."

Look at this chart. Fill in the empty spaces.

Question: What can you infer about this family from the passage?		
Clues from Passage	**What I Know**	**Inference**
• •	+ • People pick pieces of paper out of hats to help them make decisions. • Trips can be surprises. =	•

Practice It

Read this passage. Then read the questions. Circle the letter of the correct answer.

Cowhands use special clothes and supplies. From their ten-gallon hats to the spurs on their boots, each item has a purpose. The wide edge of their hats keeps out the sun and the rain. A triangle of cloth, called a bandana, keeps dust out of their mouths. The heels on their boots keep their feet from slipping out of the stirrups on their saddles. Their ropes are useful, too, for any calves that stray.

1. A ten-gallon hat is useful in places that are —

   A dusty

   B shady

   C cool

   D rainy

2. Complete this chart.

Question: What are stirrups?		
Clues from Passage • Cowhands wear boots. • Boots go into stirrups. • Stirrups are part of a saddle.	➕ **What I Know** • A saddle is a seat for riding a horse.	🟰 **Inference** •

3. What do cowhands use their ropes for?

   A to tie their hats onto their heads

   B to catch animals that wander

   C to signal to other cowhands

   D to perform rope tricks

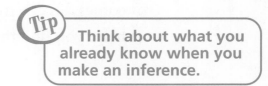

Tip Think about what you already know when you make an inference.

The Big Picture

■ Study It

All kinds of writing have facts or details. Stories have details about the characters, the action, and the setting. Other kinds of passages have facts about a topic. The facts and details in a story or passage are like clues. You can put the clues together to draw a **conclusion.** When you draw a conclusion, you see what the clues from the passage are telling you.

Read this passage.

Josie looked in the refrigerator. She looked in the cupboards. She grabbed an apple from a bowl on the counter. She said, "It's been so long since lunchtime!"

Look at this chart. It shows a conclusion you can draw.

Detail	Detail	Detail	Detail
Josie looked in the refrigerator.	Josie looked in the cupboards.	Josie grabbed an apple.	Josie said, "It's been so long since lunchtime!"

Conclusion
Josie is hungry.

Josie's actions and her statement are details that help you draw the conclusion that Josie is hungry.

A conclusion is a statement you can make from the facts and details in a passage.

- It comes directly from information in a passage.
- It helps you find the main ideas in a passage.

This page may not be reproduced without permission of Steck-Vaughn.

You can draw good conclusions if you

- look for facts and details as you read
- use the facts and details to draw conclusions

Read this passage from *Where Land Meets Sea* by Allan Fowler.

Some seashores are marshes, thick with tall reeds and other plants growing in the salty sea water. Great numbers of fish live in these salt marshes. Certain trees, such as mangroves, can grow in salt water. There are muddy seashores, too. People dig for clams in mud flats or sandy beaches. Not all beaches have fine sand . . . the sand that feels so nice and soft under your feet when you run on it. There are pebbly and stony beaches. You wouldn't want to run barefoot on one of those.

Look at this chart. Think about the facts you read. The chart shows a conclusion you can draw about seashores.

Fact	Fact	Fact	Fact
Some seashores are marshes.	Some seashores are muddy.	Some seashores have fine sand.	Some seashores are pebbly and stony.

Conclusion
There are many different kinds of seashores.

The passage tells facts about different kinds of seashores. You can use the facts to draw the conclusion that there are many different kinds of seashores.

Read this passage. What conclusion can you draw about beads?

Scientists who look for objects from the past sometimes find very old beads. Ancient Egyptians wore necklaces that looked like big collars. The necklaces were made of glass beads. In Europe glass beads and pearls were used in jewelry. They were also used to decorate clothes. Native Americans and Africans also added beads to clothes.

Look at this chart. Fill in the missing facts. Then write a conclusion.

Fact	Fact	Fact
Ancient Egyptians wore necklaces made of glass beads.		

Conclusion

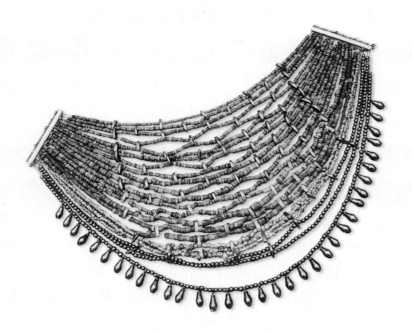

Practice It

Read this passage. Then read the questions. Circle the letter of the correct answer.

Tina and Carole moved their beds into the center of the room. Then they helped their mother paint the walls. Tina said, "Can we paint our bookcase to match the walls?"

"Yes, we should have enough paint to do that," said their mother. "And maybe I can sew some curtains, too."

"This room is going to look great," said Carole.

1. **Which room is being painted?**

   A a kitchen

   B a bedroom

   C a library

   D a sewing room

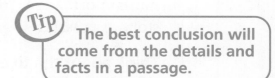

Tip The best conclusion will come from the details and facts in a passage.

2. **Look at this chart.**

Fact	Fact	Fact
Tina and Carole moved the beds in their bedroom.	Tina and Carole helped their mother paint the walls.	Tina asked to paint the bookcase.

Conclusion

What is the BEST conclusion to write in the chart? Circle the letter of the correct answer.

A Tina and Carole have painted the hallway.

B Tina and Carole read a lot of books.

C Tina and Carole are going to sew curtains.

D Tina and Carole work well together.

What's Next?

◣ Study It

When a friend tells you a story, sometimes you can guess what will happen next. You do the same thing when you read. Guessing what will happen next is called **making a prediction.**

As you read, you make predictions. Some of your predictions will be correct. Other predictions will not happen the way you thought they would. You can change your predictions as you read and get more information. You can begin predicting with the title of a story or passage.

Think about the title "Amelia Goes to Camp." What do you think this story is about?

Prediction	Clues
It is about a girl who goes to camp in the woods.	Amelia is going to camp. Camps are usually in the woods.

Remember that you can change your prediction as you read.

Read the beginning of "Amelia Goes to Camp."

> Amelia packed her uniform and her basketball. She was excited about learning new moves.

The beginning of the story shows that the first prediction was incorrect. You can make a new prediction from what you have just learned.

New Prediction	Clues
This story is about a girl who goes to basketball camp.	Amelia is packing her uniform and a basketball. She is excited about learning new moves.

Making predictions

Use It

Read this passage.

> Jackie walked down the block. She saw her best friend Jillian. Jillian was looking for her lost dog.

What will Jackie do now? Write your prediction in this chart. Then write another clue.

Prediction	Clues
	Jackie and Jillian are friends.

Practice It

Read this passage. Then make predictions. Circle the letter of the correct answer.

> Liam sat at the table. He was staring at his science book. "What's the problem?" his brother Sean asked. "We have a test tomorrow. I don't understand this," Liam said. "Let me take a look. I always liked fourth-grade science," Sean said.

1. **What will happen next?**

   A Liam will get a snack.

   B Liam will close the book.

   C Sean will leave the room.

   D Sean will help Liam study.

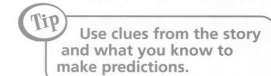

Tip Use clues from the story and what you know to make predictions.

2. **What is Liam probably thinking?**

   A "My poor big brother."

   B "I want to ride my bike."

   C "I'm lucky Sean is willing to help me."

   D "I need to call my friends."

Prove It!

◢ Study It

When you draw a conclusion or make an inference about a story or passage, you are thinking about what you have read. You use the details and facts in the passage to draw conclusions. You can also use the details and facts, along with information you already know, to make inferences. The details and facts plus your own knowledge are the **supporting information** for your conclusions and inferences.

To draw a conclusion, put together the details or facts in a passage. Ask yourself, *What do the details or facts in this passage tell me?*

Read this passage. Then look at the chart. It shows supporting information for a conclusion you can draw.

> Marcus and Jamal were walking to school one morning. They carried their book bags and lunches. Marcus said, "I'm always sad to leave summer vacation behind."
>
> Jamal said, "Me, too. But think about seeing the friends we haven't seen in a while. There may be new kids and teachers to meet, too."

Conclusion	Supporting Information
Marcus and Jamal are good friends.	<u>Details from the passage</u>: The boys are walking to school together. They are talking about their feelings. Jamal is offering Marcus encouragement.

Good friends like to spend time together. They often share their feelings with each other and offer encouragement. You can conclude that Marcus and Jamal are good friends.

These steps will help you draw a conclusion.

Step 1	Step 2	Step 3	Step 4
Underline important facts and details.	Think about what the facts and details tell you.	Put together the facts and details to draw a conclusion.	Check your conclusion against the passage.

Support from text

Using the clues in a passage and your own knowledge helps you make inferences and find missing information. An inference answers the question, *What information is missing from this passage?*

Read this passage. Then look at the chart. It shows the supporting information for an inference you can make.

Vera and Kristin were blowing up balloons in the kitchen. Kristin was trying to tie a balloon full of air. She accidentally let go of the balloon. The girls started to laugh. "Did you see that?" Vera asked.

Conclusion	Supporting Information
Kristin's balloon flew around the kitchen.	<u>Detail from the passage:</u> Kristin accidentally let go of the balloon. <u>What I know:</u> Balloons fly around when they release air.

Kristin is blowing up a balloon when she accidentally lets it go. You know that balloons fly around when they release air. You can make the inference that Kristin's balloon flew around the kitchen.

These steps will help you use supporting information to make an inference.

Step 1	Step 2	Step 3	Step 4
As you read, underline important facts and details in the passage.	Then think about what you already know about the topic of the passage.	Use all of this information to make an inference.	Check to be sure that the facts and details in the passage support your inference.

Use It

Read this passage from *Pluto* by Dennis Brindell Fradin. Look for clues that help you draw conclusions and make inferences.

Have you ever looked at the sky on a clear night? If so, you have seen many twinkling points of light. They are called stars.

The nighttime stars look like points of light because they are so very far away from us. In fact, stars are giant balls of hot, glowing gas. The hottest stars are blue-white. Their surfaces are at a temperature of over 55,000°F. If our world were that hot, it would soon burn up. The red stars are the "coolest." Their surfaces are at a temperature of about 5,500°F, which is still plenty hot.

Look at this chart. Add supporting information for the conclusion.

Conclusion	Supporting Information
The temperature of stars affects their color.	Details from the passage:

Now, complete this chart by adding the inference.

Inferences	Supporting Information
	Details from the passage: Twinkling points of light are called stars. Stars are giant balls of hot, glowing gas.
	What I Know: The blue flame on a gas stove is very hot.

Practice It

Read this passage.

Mr. Lampton led his class to a stream. "Fossils show us what things used to look like. Maybe a leaf fell in the mud. The mud turned into a rock. The leaf washed away. But the mark of the leaf stayed. Let's see what we can find here." The children started turning over rocks.

Junie called out, "Mr. Lampton, could a fossil look like a bug carved into a rock?"

"Let me see. You have good eyes, Junie!"

1. **Look at this chart. What is the BEST conclusion to write? Circle the letter of the correct answer.**

Conclusion	Supporting Information
	Details from the passage: Fossils are made from mud and leaves, animals, and insects that have turned into rock. The children are turning over rocks.

A The students are looking for a stream.

B The students are looking for rocks.

C The students are looking for bugs.

D The students are looking for fossils.

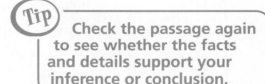
Tip
Check the passage again to see whether the facts and details support your inference or conclusion.

2. **Look at this chart. What is the BEST supporting information to write? Circle the letter of the correct answer.**

Inference	Supporting Information
Junie found a fossil.	Details from the passage:

A Junie was near a stream and found a rock.

B Junie described a rock, and Mr. Lampton praised her.

C Mr. Lampton described how a fossil is made.

D Mr. Lampton's example included a leaf.

Making Connections

◣ Study It

Different reading materials, or **sources,** offer different information about a subject. For example, in school you might read a social studies book about the election process. At home you might read a newspaper article about someone who is running for president. In the park you might read a story about a girl who wants to be the president of the United States when she grows up.

When you read about a subject in two or more sources, you should compare and contrast the sources. Ask yourself these questions.

- What is the same about these sources?
- What is different about them?

Read these passages. Then look at the chart that shows what is the same and what is different about the passages.

Passage 1

Sally looked at the pictures she had taken. She was disappointed with them. "Why does this picture look so dark? I can barely see the decorations we worked so hard on!"

Passage 2

Photographs are pictures taken with cameras. Photographs record how light falls on an object. If an object is too dark, it will not reflect light. The picture will turn out dark. If there is too much light, the opposite might happen. The picture will have too much light.

Passage 1	Both Passages	Passage 2
• story about Sally • one character • talks about feelings	• topic is photographs • talk about the darkness of photographs	• explains how light affects photographs • no characters • no feelings

Connections

Read the first passage from *Mei Li* by Thomas Handforth and the second passage from *Chinese New Year* by Catherine Chambers. Notice what is the same and what is different about them.

Passage 1

Inside the house on the morning before New Year's Day, everyone was very busy. Mei Li, a little girl with a candle-top pigtail, was scrubbing and sweeping and dusting. Her mother, Mrs. Wang, was baking and frying and chopping. Her brother, San Yu, was fixing and tasting and mixing. A fine feast was being prepared for the Kitchen God, who would come out at midnight to every family in China to tell them what they must do during the coming year.

Passage 2

Not many people go to bed on New Year's Eve. The streets buzz with happy people, young and old alike. Temples are full of worshipers. Families gather from far and wide to eat a special meal together.

Now look at this chart. It shows how you can compare the passages.

Passage 1	Both Passages	Passage 2
• story about Chinese family • three characters • set in the morning	• talk about Chinese New Year's celebration • talk about the special meal	• true description • characters are general people • set at night

When you make connections between passages,

- read each passage carefully
- notice what is different between the passages
- notice what is the same about the passages
- compare the organization and style of writing
- compare the characters, the setting, and the action

◣ Use It

Read these passages. Notice what is the same and what is different about them.

Passage 1

The sun was setting behind the statue. Agnes caught her breath. The statue was the most beautiful thing she had ever seen. She had read about the statue. She had no idea how she would feel when she finally saw it. Some people said it was green and ugly. All Agnes saw was the beautiful torch and the statue's crown. She knew her long journey was almost over. She would be in New York soon. She would be in the United States.

Passage 2

The Statue of Liberty is a large statue. The statue is of a woman wearing a crown and carrying a torch. It stands on an island in Upper New York Bay. The statue was a gift to the United States from France in the 1800s. When people arrive in New York by boat, the statue is one of the first things that they see.

Now look at this chart. Fill in the empty spaces to show how the passages are the same and different.

Passage 1	Both Passages	Passage 2
• story about Agnes	•	•
•		• no characters
•	• immigrants see statue when they arrive in New York City	• no thought or feelings
		•
• uses many adjectives	•	

Tip: When you compare two passages, look at all the parts of each passage.

Practice It

Read these passages. Then look at the chart. Read the question. Circle the letter of the correct answer.

Passage 1

Amanda loved Uncle Fred. She thought he was amazing because he played the fiddle so well. When he came to visit, she could not wait until he opened the old black case. He let her put the rosin, a chalky powder, on the bow. Then he tuned the fiddle. Finally, he tapped his foot and played the fiddle as Amanda sang.

Passage 2

Fiddles are stringed instruments. They are played with a bow. They are sometimes called violins. Fiddles are used to play anything from very formal music to simple country songs. It takes years to learn to play the fiddle well. Fiddles are easily carried, so music can be made anywhere.

Passage 1	Both Passages	Passage 2
• story about Amanda and Uncle Fred • fiddle is played •	• topic is fiddles • talk about fiddle bows	• gives facts about fiddles • describes a fiddle •

1. **Which item belongs in the Passage 1 box?**

   A characters talk to each other

   B talks about one character's feelings and thoughts

   C three characters

   D describes how characters look

2. **Which item belongs in the Passage 2 box?**

   A talks about types of fiddles

   B talks about types of fiddle bows

   C talks about types of fiddle music

   D talks about types of fiddle players

Unit 3
Test-Taking Strategy

Strategy: Use Details

In this unit you learned how to draw conclusions, make inferences, support your conclusions and inferences, and compare and contrast two passages. On tests you will see questions that ask you to use these skills.

Read the question and each answer choice carefully. If you cannot decide between two answer choices, go back to the passage. Look for the choice that agrees with the passage.

Try It Out

Read this passage. Choose the answer that is the BEST inference for the passage. Circle the letter of the correct answer.

> Bess and her mother prepared for their trip. They packed a picnic lunch, swimsuits, and towels. "Don't forget your sandals. The sand might be really hot!" Bess's mother said.

Bess and her mother are probably going to the —

A swimming pool

B desert

C mountains

D beach

You can rule out answers by looking at the details in the passage. Bess's mother says that the sand might be hot. There is not usually sand at a swimming pool, so **A** is not a good answer. You do not swim in the desert, so **B** is not a good answer. Sand is not usually a problem in the mountains, so **C** is not a good answer. All of the items Bess and her mother pack can be used at the beach, so **D** is the best answer.

Unit 3 • Putting Ideas Together
Put It to the Test

This test will check what you have learned in this unit.

DIRECTIONS: Read these passages. Then read the items. Circle the letters of the correct answers.

Flags

Flags have been used since ancient times. Flags are usually made of cloth. They are usually rectangles. Flags are most often used to identify a country or a group. For example, flags can be used in a parade to name the group marching behind the flag. Flags are also used as signals. In car races, flags tell drivers when to go fast or slow. At sea, flags are used to send messages from one ship to another. Sometimes flags are given as rewards for good work. Flags are often put on poles so that people can see them easily.

Jason's Project

Jason was working at the table. He was drawing on a piece of paper. "That looks nice. What is it?" his father asked.

"My friends and I are going to ride our bikes in the parade. I'm making a flag for us. It's fun to make things."

"How will you carry the flag?"

"I have a pole for it. Can you help me put the pole on my bike when I'm done drawing this?" said Jason.

"Sure, and I can't wait to see how this looks in the parade!"

1. **Why would flags usually be made in the same way?**

   A Flag makers are lazy.

   B There are not enough flag makers to make different flags.

   C It makes flags easy to use in many different places.

   D It is the law.

2. **Why would flags be a popular way to identify a country or group?**

   A They are large and easily seen.

   B Many people make flags.

   C They are colorful and beautiful.

   D They are easy to put on poles.

GO ON

Achieve It! Practice Cards

_____

3. Flags are used in races —

   A to add color

   B to show history

   C for safety

   D as prizes for winners

4. Why would flags be used to send messages at sea?

   A Ships do not have telephones.

   B There is no mail service.

   C Ships do not have computers.

   D They can be seen easily across distances.

5. What inference can you make about Jason?

   A He has a new bike.

   B He likes art projects.

   C He is worried about the parade.

   D He needs to plan his flag better.

6. Which detail supports the conclusion that Jason's father is helpful?

   A He wants to see the parade.

   B He likes Jason's work.

   C He will help Jason put the flag on the bike.

   D He asks many questions.

7. Jason and his friends are using the flag —

   A to identify their group

   B to win a prize

   C to show that they can go fast

   D to send a message to another group

8. How is Jason's flag different from most of the flags mentioned in the first passage?

   A It will be in a parade.

   B It is being made at home.

   C It will be on a pole.

   D It is made out of paper.

9. How is the passage on Jason's project different from the passage on flags?

   A It tells how to make a flag.

   B It tells how flags are used to identify groups.

   C It explains that flags are usually carried.

   D It tells about two characters, Jason and his father.

GO ON

Achieve It! Practice Cards

Window Gardens

Even if you do not have much space outdoors, you can still grow a small garden. You can make a window garden. Window gardens are grown in boxes. The boxes are made of wood or plastic. They are attached beneath a window. Most window gardens contain flowers. To pick plants for a window garden, think about how much sunlight the plants will get. Then ask someone at a garden store to help you choose plants. In no time your window will be alive with growth!

Delia's Surprise

Delia wanted to make a surprise for her father. He liked pepper plants, so she decided to make him a window garden. She and her brother worked to make a wooden box. They found dirt to put in it. With her mother's help, Delia picked out and planted some seeds. Delia and her brother watered the seeds and watched them grow. Just in time for Father's Day, the first small pepper appeared. When Delia gave her father the box, he was excited. He said, "Where can we put this great garden? How about next to the kitchen window? Then we can harvest our dinner without even going outside!"

10. **The author of "Window Gardens" thinks that window gardens are —**

   A troublesome

   B expensive

   C useful

   D enjoyable

11. **What is one of the MOST important things to consider when making a window garden?**

   A finding space in a garden

   B choosing plants for it

   C finding dirt for it

   D picking a shape for it

Achieve It! Practice Cards

_____

12. Why do most window gardens contain flowers?

   A Flowers attract bees and other insects.

   B Flowers are often eaten in salads and other dishes.

   C Flowers can be cut and given away as gifts.

   D Flowers are small, smell good, and are pretty to look at.

13. Which of these BEST describes the gift for Delia's father?

   A a family project

   B an indoor present

   C an expensive present

   D a beautiful sight

14. What will Delia's family do with the peppers?

   A eat them

   B give them to neighbors

   C sell them at a stand

   D save them for the winter

15. Delia's window garden is different because it —

   A was next to a kitchen

   B needed lots of water

   C contained pepper plants

   D was made of wood

16. Delia's choice of plants for her father's window garden shows that she is —

   A thoughtful

   B rude

   C forgetful

   D funny

17. Delia's father is excited when he gets his gift because —

   A he does not like the gift

   B he likes the gift

   C he plans to return the gift

   D he plans to give Delia a gift

18. Delia's window box is made of wood. She could also have used a box made of —

   A foil

   B rock

   C plastic

   D paper

19. The passage on window gardens and the passage on Delia's surprise both tell about —

   A fun ways to enjoy plants

   B the price of window boxes

   C a Father's Day celebration

   D people and their feelings

Achieve It! **Practice Cards**

Unit 4
Parts and Patterns

It All Fits Together

Have you ever seen something that is in pieces, and then watched someone put it together? At first, it looks like a mess. But soon you begin to understand the way the parts match up.

In this unit you will learn how writers gather their ideas into neat patterns and then group those ideas into sections to make a book. You will also learn about sections in a book that tell you how a book is arranged.

Lesson 18

First, Next, and Finally

■ Study It

Writers use patterns to make their ideas clear to the reader. One pattern that writers often use is **sequence.** Sequence, or time order, is the order in which events happen or the order in which steps in a process are explained.

If you are making a sandwich, think about what you do first. What do you do next? Putting ideas or steps in proper order helps you understand the sequence.

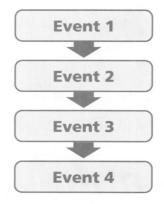

Signal words can tell you the order in which things happen. For sequence, look for time-order words such as <u>later</u>, <u>before</u>, <u>first</u>, second, <u>next</u>, last, <u>finally</u>, <u>after</u>, <u>then</u>, and <u>now</u>.

> **<u>First</u>, Sandra wrote a shopping list. <u>Then</u>, she went to the store.**

The words <u>first</u> and <u>Then</u> show you when each event happened.

Some signal words, such as <u>yesterday</u>, <u>noon</u>, <u>tomorrow</u>, <u>last month</u>, <u>in June</u>, or <u>in 1942</u>, are more exact.

> **Carl wrote a three-page paper <u>last Thursday</u>.**

The words <u>last Thursday</u> show exactly when the event happened.

Sometimes writers do not use signal words when they tell a story or explain a process. You will need to use what you already know to follow the sequence of events if time-order words are not used.

Diagram:
Event 1 → Event 2 → Event 3 → Event 4

Read these directions for making a treat. Look at the boxes to follow the order of the steps in the directions. Notice how the signal words first, then, now, and next are used in the passage.

It is easy to make a great, healthful treat. First, wash your hands well. Then, get out cornflakes, two bananas, and a small container of yogurt. Put the cornflakes into a plastic bag and crush them with a rolling pin. Now, put the crushed cereal into a pie tin. Next, peel the bananas. Dip each whole banana in the yogurt. Roll the bananas in the cereal until they are completely coated. Place the coated bananas on a tray lined with waxed paper. Put the bananas in the freezer. Wait three hours, and then enjoy your treat!

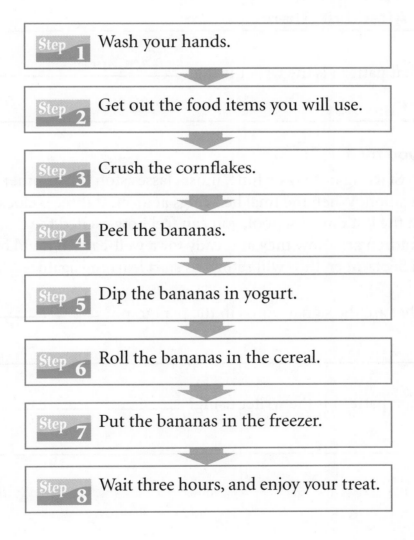

Step 1 Wash your hands.

Step 2 Get out the food items you will use.

Step 3 Crush the cornflakes.

Step 4 Peel the bananas.

Step 5 Dip the bananas in yogurt.

Step 6 Roll the bananas in the cereal.

Step 7 Put the bananas in the freezer.

Step 8 Wait three hours, and enjoy your treat.

Use It

Read the passage and underline the signal words. Then read the questions and write your answers on the lines. Look at these examples.

To get to Marcela's house from school, first make a left turn on Worthington Avenue. After that, go two blocks. Then, make a second left onto Smithfield Avenue. When you come to the third stoplight, you are at Essex Road. Turn right. Marcela lives at 1980 Essex Road.

1. What are the signal words in the paragraph? _____first,_____

_____After that, Then_____

2. What pattern is the writer using? _____sequence, or_____

_____time order_____

Now you try it.

Starting in May or June, most classes stop for summer vacation. When the final bell rings at around three o'clock on the last day of school, you can feel how excited the children are. Now they are ready for a well-earned holiday. In September, they will return to start learning again.

3. What are the signal words in the paragraph? _____

_____

4. What pattern is the writer using? _____

_____

Practice It

Read this passage. Then read the items. Circle the letter of the correct answer.

The year was 1608. By now strangers lived by the river. When my mother sent me to gather berries, I didn't mean to go near the people.

I didn't notice the girl come near until it was too late. Suddenly we were face to face. We stared at each other. Finally she smiled, and I smiled back. Then I gave her some berries. She handed me a ribbon.

"Sarah, where are you?" a man called as he came up the hill.

The girl put a finger to her lips, turned around, and walked slowly toward the man. At last, I slipped away through the brush.

1. **What happened first?**

   A The child telling the story was sent to get berries.

   B Strangers built homes near the river.

   C The child telling the story walked many miles to the river.

   D A strange girl was holding a ribbon.

2. **What signal words tell you that the author used sequence in the second paragraph?**

   A Finally, Then

   B back, up

   C stared, smiled

   D Suddenly, near

 Tip Signal words help you recognize the order of steps and events.

Before You Read

Study It

Knowing the parts of a book will help you locate information quickly and easily. The first page you are likely to see is the **title page.**

The title page tells you important information. It shows you the book **title** and the **author,** or the person who wrote the book. It also names the **illustrator,** or the person who did the art for the book. The **publisher,** or the company that printed the book, and the **city** where the book was published are also on the title page.

The next part you see is called the **table of contents.** This part lists the **chapters,** or main topics, in the book. If the book is a collection of stories, the table of contents tells you the names of the stories. It also lists the page numbers on which the chapters or stories begin. Most important, it gives the order of the contents in the book.

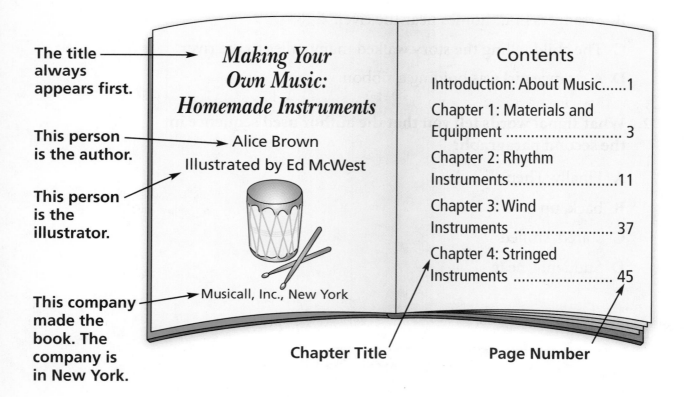

The title always appears first.

This person is the author.

This person is the illustrator.

This company made the book. The company is in New York.

Making Your Own Music: Homemade Instruments

Alice Brown

Illustrated by Ed McWest

Musicall, Inc., New York

Contents

Introduction: About Music......1

Chapter 1: Materials and Equipment 3

Chapter 2: Rhythm Instruments....................11

Chapter 3: Wind Instruments 37

Chapter 4: Stringed Instruments 45

Chapter Title

Page Number

TOC/title page

Use It

Use the title page and table of contents on page 78 to answer the questions. Write your answers on the lines. Look at these examples.

1. Who is the author of the book? ___Alice Brown___

2. Where could you MOST LIKELY find information on how to make a drum? ___Chapter 2: Rhythm Instruments___

Now you try it.

1. What is the title of the book? _____

_____

2. Which chapter would probably tell you what supplies you need to make strings for a guitar? _____

_____

Practice It

Read the title page and table of contents on page 78. Then read the items. Circle the letter of the correct answer.

1. **Who is the publisher of the book?**

   A Ed McWest

   B Musicall, Inc.

   C New York

   D Alice Brown

2. **Where are you likely to find directions for making a flute?**

   A Chapter 1

   B Chapter 2

   C Chapter 3

   D Chapter 4

Tip Use the table of contents as a guide to help find information in a book.

It Stands Out from All the Rest!

■ **Study It**

Most authors use **headings** to make their writing easier to understand. Headings are like titles. They tell you what information a section or paragraph contains.

Read this passage.

> ### Growing Potatoes
>
> Growing potatoes is easy if you follow these simple rules.
>
> **Get Ready**
> You need several nine-inch pots with holes in the bottom, good soil, and seed potatoes.
>
> **Get Started**
> Put the potatoes in a light, cool place.
>
> Wait for the eyes to send out little green shoots.
>
> **Plant**
> Fill each pot about one-third full with potting soil.
>
> Put the sprouted potatoes in the pots. Cover the potatoes with two to three inches of soil. Add enough water to make the soil damp, but not wet. Wait for green leaves to appear.

This passage has three headings: Get Ready, Get Started, and Plant. They divide the passage into sections and give you a clue to what each section is about.

Headings help you identify the section or paragraph that has the information you need.

Headings are often written in larger, **boldface** type. Sometimes they are underlined. Some the authors use *italics,* or slanted letters. These styles make headings and words stand out on the page.

Authors usually label large topics with headings in a large-size type. Then, under those headings, they label smaller topics with subheadings in a medium-size type. These smaller headings are called subheadings.

Headings and typeface

Use It

Look at the passage headings on page 80 to answer the questions. Write your answers on the lines. First, look at the example.

Containers for Plants

Pots Plastic pots are inexpensive. They come in many colors and sizes. Wooden containers need care so that the wood will not rot. Many growers prefer clay pots.

Window boxes The best window boxes are made of plastic or clay. They come in many sizes. Think about where you want to use a window box. Then you can decide which size is best.

Containers for
plants What is the passage about?

Now you try it.

_____ 1. Which heading says something about the cost of containers?

_____ 2. What kind of type do the headings use?

Practice It

Look at the passage above. Then read the items. Circle the letter of the correct answer.

1. **The heading "Containers for Plants" tells you that the passage is about —**

   A plastic pots

   B wooden containers

   C different kinds of containers

   D clay pots

2. **What is the topic of the second paragraph?**

   A containers for plants

   B growing plants in pots

   C boxes and barrels

   D window boxes

 Tip Use headings to help you locate information in a passage quickly.

This page may not be reproduced without permission of Steck-Vaughn.

Like a Guide Book

Lesson 21

Study It

The **index** appears at the back of the book. An index tells you which pages of the book have the information that you need.

The information in an index is organized into **topics,** or single ideas that are discussed in the book. Topics in the index are written in alphabetical, or *ABC,* order.

Below a topic you might find **subtopics.** Subtopics are ideas that are part of a larger topic. Page numbers follow the topics and subtopics. Numbers separated by a dash, such as 67–73, mean that information begins on page 67 and ends on page 73. Single pages separated by commas, such as 67, 70, 74, mean that information is on each of those pages.

Look at this index from an art book.

> **Drawing board,** 4
>
> **Erasers,** 5
>
> **Paints,** 26–35
>   acrylic paints, 26–29; oil paints, 31–32;
>   poster paints, 30; watercolors, 33–35
>
> **Paper,** 36–38
>   drawing, 36; poster, 36; construction, 37–38
>
> **Pencils,** 7, 39

The topics are sometimes in **boldface,** or darker type. To find out about erasers, turn to page 5. The topic of paints is covered on pages 26–35. Poster paints is a subtopic. To find out about poster paints, look on page 30. You could find information about pencils on two different pages, 7 and 39.

Sometimes you might not find the topic you want in an index. Think of another way to say the topic. For example, suppose that you want to learn how to draw squares. But you cannot find squares in the index. Look under the topic shapes. Squares may be a subtopic there.

Index

Use It

Use the index on page 82 to answer the questions. Look for the topics and subtopics. Write your answers on the lines.

____subtopic____   Is <u>poster paints</u> a topic or a subtopic?

Now you try it.

_____ 1. Where would you find information about watercolor paints?

_____ 2. What two subtopics about paper are on
_____   page 36?

Practice It

Read this index. Then read the items. Circle the letter of the correct answer.

> **Chalk,** 7–8
>
> **Circles and cubes,** 9–11
>
> **Colors,** 12–25
> combining, 14–19; mixing of, 20, 22, 24; primary, 12, 14, 25

1. **Which page would give you information about combining colors?**

    A page 12

    B page 15

    C page 20

    D page 24

2. **On what page would you find information about circles?**

    A page 6

    B page 8

    C page 10

    D page 13

Tip An index is a quick and easy guide to find the information you need.

Unit 4
Test-Taking Strategy

Strategy: Look for the Signals

In this unit you learned that writers give signals to help you understand what you read.

- Signal words, such as <u>first</u>, <u>next</u>, <u>last</u>, <u>yesterday</u>, or <u>next month</u>
- Headings
- **Boldface type**
- <u>Underlining</u>
- *Italics,* or slanted letters
- Colored print
- CAPITALIZATION

You also learned that books give you signals, too. The title page and table of contents tell you what the book is about. The index tells you where to find information.

Try It Out

Read the passage. Then answer the question. Circle the letter of the correct answer.

> Think of your favorite fairy tale. How could the ending be different? Start in the middle of the story. Then write a new ending.

Which of these words from the passage is a signal word?

A Think

B How

C Write

D Then

<u>Think</u> and <u>write</u> are words that tell you what to do. <u>How</u> is a question word. <u>Then</u> is a signal word that shows time order. So, the correct answer is **D, Then.**

Unit 4 • Parts and Patterns
Put It to the Test

This test will check what you have learned in this unit.

DIRECTIONS: Read the title page and table of contents. Then read each item. Circle the letter of the correct answer.

FUN
ACTIVITIES
FOR SUMMER DAYS

Tom Claussen and Sue Cook

Illustrated by Mary Long

Summertime Press, New York

Contents

1. **Who drew the pictures in the book?**

   A Tom Claussen

   B Sue Cook

   C Mary Long

   D Summertime Press

2. **In which chapter would you probably find recipes?**

   A Paper Projects

   B Using Cans and Jars

   C Good Enough to Eat

   D Materials

3. **If you wanted to make something from pine cones, which chapter would you probably read?**

   A Painting Fun

   B Games and Puzzles

   C Making Music

   D The Great Outdoors

GO ON

Achieve It! Practice Cards

_____

DIRECTIONS: Look at the index. Then read each item. Circle the letter of the correct answer.

INDEX

Brushes, types of, 72

Cans, 27–30

Cardboard, 4, 6, 7, 10

Crossword puzzles, 49, 51

Drawing paper, 3, 5, 9

Drums, 65

Foods, 35–46
breads, 35–37; muffins, 38–40; snacks, 41; yogurt smoothies, 42–46

Jars, 31–34

Jigsaw puzzles, 48

Paints, kinds of, 15–16

Tools, 72–76

4. **Which of these topics has subtopics?**

   A jars

   B cans

   C foods

   D tools

5. **On which of these pages would you look to find out what kind of can to use?**

   A page 5

   B page 6

   C page 31

   D page 35

DIRECTIONS: Read this passage. Then read each item. Circle the letter of the correct answer.

What Should I Do Today?

Summer days can seem long and dull. Now you'll never again have to say, "There's nothing to do!" The first things you need are some paper, glue, and a bit of imagination!

6. **You can tell that the word imagination is important because it is —**

   A slanted

   B in capital letters

   C underlined

   D in dark print

7. **The heading tells you that the passage is probably about —**

   A painting a poster

   B finding things to do

   C drawing a picture

   D making things with paper

8. **Which of these is a signal word in the paragraph?**

   A Summer

   B long

   C glue

   D first

STOP

Achieve It! Practice Cards

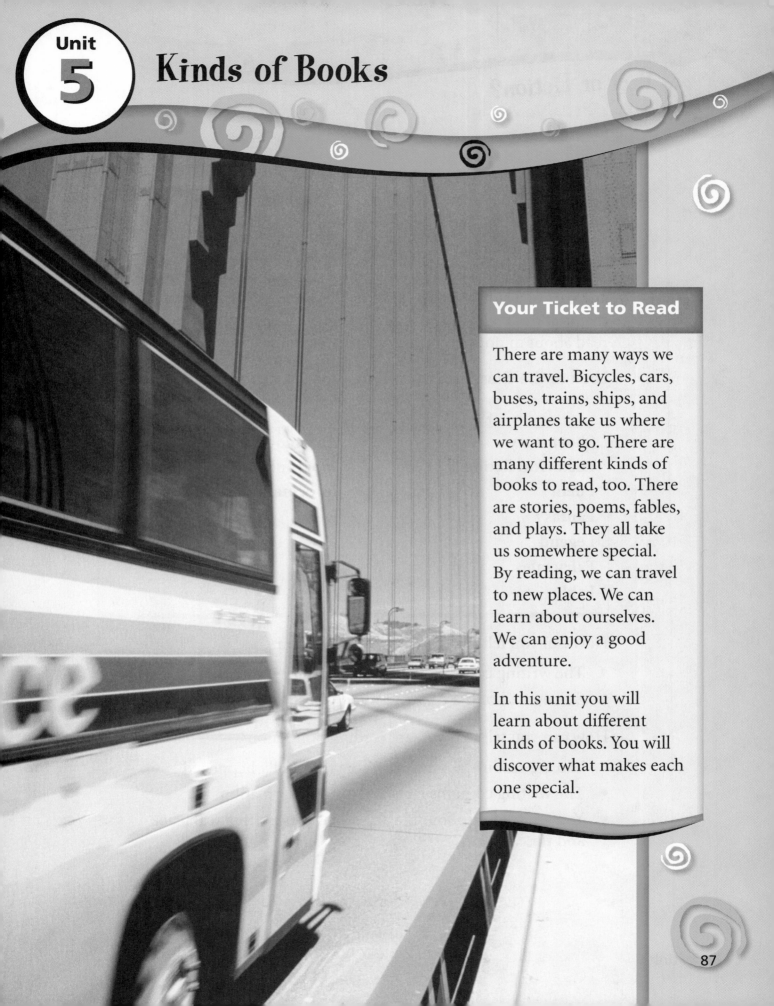

Kinds of Books

Your Ticket to Read

There are many ways we can travel. Bicycles, cars, buses, trains, ships, and airplanes take us where we want to go. There are many different kinds of books to read, too. There are stories, poems, fables, and plays. They all take us somewhere special. By reading, we can travel to new places. We can learn about ourselves. We can enjoy a good adventure.

In this unit you will learn about different kinds of books. You will discover what makes each one special.

Fact or Fiction?

◢ Study It

Why do you read? Sometimes you read for fun, and sometimes you read to learn.

Most writing fits into two groups, fiction and nonfiction. **Fiction** is writing that comes from an author's imagination. It can be based on facts, or on real people, or even on real experiences. However, if any part of a story is make-believe, it is fiction. **Nonfiction** is writing that is about real people, places, things, or ideas. Everything that you read about in nonfiction is true or has actually happened in real life.

Look at the chart. It shows some types of fiction and nonfiction.

Fiction	Nonfiction
Short story	**Autobiography**
Historical fiction	**Biography**
Poem	**Informational text**
Fantasy	**Essay**
Legend	
Fairy tale	
Fable	

How can you tell that you are reading fiction?

- The writing comes from the author's imagination.
- Some or all of the characters and places are make-believe.

How can you tell that you are reading nonfiction?

- You are reading about something that really happened.
- The writing contains facts and other information.
- You are reading about a real person or event in a real place and time.

Fiction/nonfiction

Read this passage. Then look at the chart. Use the chart to decide whether the passage is fiction or nonfiction.

Animals have different ways of hiding from other animals and people. The color of an animal is one thing that can help it hide. An animal may have a body color that matches the color of its surroundings, or where it lives. For example, the green grasshopper stays well-hidden in the grass. Also, the copperhead snake has bands of orange and brown that help it stay hidden on the ground. The snake looks just like the fallen leaves. Some animals actually change color to match the things around them. The arctic fox is one such animal. In spring the fox's fur is brown, to help the animal blend into its surroundings. But in winter, the fox's fur is white, to match the snow.

Fiction or Nonfiction?	
Fiction	**Nonfiction**
It comes from the author's imagination.	What happens is real.
The characters, actions, or settings are make-believe.	There are facts and other information.
The characters, actions, or settings can be real, but other parts are make-believe.	It is about real people, places, or things.

According to the information in the chart, the passage is nonfiction. It gives facts about real animals. In real life, grasshoppers do blend in with their surroundings. The facts about copperhead snakes are true, too. The arctic fox really is able to survive because of its protective color. Nothing in this passage is make-believe.

Read this passage from "Pearl" by Debby Atwell. Look for parts that are real and parts that are make-believe.

At night, when the house is quiet, I look out my bedroom window and see only stars above the dark trees. It's then that I remember family events all the way back to when this country began.

My grandfather told me that when he was just a small boy, he rode in a big parade with the first president of the United States. It was down Wall Street, New York City, on Inauguration Day. Grandfather said George Washington scooped him up just like that out of the crowd and carried him on his horse while everybody cheered. He felt that he was the luckiest person alive.

Is this passage nonfiction or fiction? Use this checklist to find out. Circle <u>real</u>, <u>make-believe</u>, or <u>both</u> after each question.

1. What are the characters in this passage?

   real   make-believe   both

2. What are the events in this passage?

   real   make-believe   both

3. What is the setting in this passage?

   real   make-believe   both

Now circle your answer to this question.

4. Is this passage an example of fiction or nonfiction?

   fiction   nonfiction

Practice It

Read the passage. Then read the items. Circle the letter of the correct answer.

Many people think that all sharks are large, man-eating creatures. But not all sharks are like the great white shark. Even the largest shark, the whale shark, is not thought to be harmful to people. In fact, there are more than 300 kinds of sharks, and they come in many interesting sizes and shapes. The dwarf shark is only about six to ten inches long. Angel sharks do not look like sharks at all because they are almost flat. The zebra shark has patterns like stripes on its skin. The hammerhead shark may be the strangest-looking shark. Its head looks like a hammer, and it has eyes on each end of the "hammer."

1. **This passage is nonfiction because it —**

   A tells about make-believe animals

   B takes place in a make-believe setting

   C gives facts

   D comes from the author's imagination

2. **To write this passage, the author would first need to —**

   A have a good imagination

   B read a short story about sharks

   C see a real shark

   D study sharks

3. **You would probably find this passage in a book called —**

   A *Ocean Plants*

   B *Sammy, the Shark*

   C *All About Sharks*

   D *What's in the Fish Tank?*

Tip If any part of the story you are reading is make-believe, you are reading fiction.

Real People/Real Stories

◢ Study It

Biographies and **autobiographies** are true stories about people's lives. An author writes a biography about someone else's life. An author writes an autobiography about his or her own life.

Look at the chart. It shows examples of the titles of a biography and of an autobiography.

Biography	Autobiography
If a Bus Could Talk: The Story of Rosa Parks, by Faith Ringgold	*Rosa Parks: My Story,* by Rosa Parks

Biographies and autobiographies are alike because both are true stories about a person. That person is called the **subject.** However, if the subject writes the story, it is an autobiography. If someone else writes the story, it is a biography.

Both biographies and autobiographies are usually told in time order, or the order in which events actually happened. But sometimes the author may skip back and forth between the past and the present. This helps the author show how the events are related.

Biographies and autobiographies contain information about real people and events. However, the author of an autobiography has information that the writer of a biography does not. The author of an autobiography can remember feelings or thoughts that he or she had in the past. The author of a biography must use information from things like letters, books, and **interviews.** Interviews are talks with the subject or people who have known the subject.

Biography/autobiography

Use It

Use what you have learned to answer each question.
Write biography, autobiography, or both on the lines. Look
at these examples.

_____biography_____ 1. Interviews are a source of information.

_____both_____ 2. The author tells events in the order in which they happened.

Now you try it.

_____ 1. The author uses his or her own thoughts and feelings.

_____ 2. It is a true story of someone's life.

_____ 3. The author tells the story of someone else's life.

Practice It

Read each question. Circle the letter of the correct answer.

1. **If you wrote your autobiography, which of the following would make the BEST title?**

   A *My Friend Ralph*

   B *My Grandfather*

   C *My Life As I Remember It*

   D *Memories of Fourth Grade*

2. **The author of a biography would probably find which source useful?**

   A a dictionary

   B the subject's letters

   C a television commercial

   D recipes by the subject

Tip

Autobiographies usually include the author's feelings and thoughts.

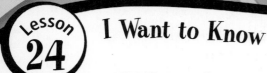

I Want to Know

◢ Study It

Have you ever wanted to find out more about something? Maybe you needed to learn more about dog care. Maybe you wanted to know why the planet Mars is red. Or maybe you wanted to learn to ride a skateboard safely. If so, you would probably look for information in books such as these:

- *Dogs: How to Care for and Understand Them*
- *Learn More About the Planets*
- *Skateboard Safety*

These books are part of a group called **informational texts.** Informational texts explain and give facts about something. They can be written about almost any subject.

Look at the chart. It shows some of the different types of informational texts.

Types of Informational Texts	
Textbooks	Magazines
Newspapers	Signs
Reference Books	Flyers

In good informational texts, the author—

- uses facts that have been checked for accuracy, with no important facts left out
- writes the information so that the reader can understand it

Read this passage.

John Philip Sousa wrote "The Stars and Stripes Forever" in 1897. Not many people know that Sousa wrote this famous march while on a boat, without the help of a single musical instrument! The tune is now the official march of the United States. In 1997, one hundred years after Sousa completed the piece, a special United States postage stamp was created to honor this march.

You can tell that this passage is an informational text because it gives you facts about John Philip Sousa and explains the history of "The Stars and Stripes Forever."

Informational texts

◢ Use It

Use what you have learned about informational texts to decide whether each statement below is true or false. Write your answers on the lines. Look at these examples.

_____true_____ 1. Informational texts explain and give facts.

_____true_____ 2. Informational texts are written so that the reader can understand them.

Now you try it.

_____ 1. Fiction books are a kind of informational text.

_____ 2. The facts in an informational text have been checked for accuracy.

_____ 3. It is all right to leave some important facts out of an informational text.

◢ Practice It

Read each question. Circle the letter of the correct answer.

1. **Which of these is a title of an informational text?**

   A *Beauty and the Beast*

   B *The Lives of Fairies*

   C *How Computers Work*

   D *Fluffy, the Kitten*

2. **If you wanted to learn about whales, which book would probably be the BEST source of information?**

   A *Under the Ocean*

   B *Humphrey, the Lost Whale*

   C *My First Fishing Trip*

   D *Whales: Strange and Wonderful*

 Tip Choose an informational text to learn more about a topic.

Imagine That!

◢ Study It

Fantasy is a special kind of fiction. It involves things that never happen in real life. Fantasies contain magical events and unusual characters, such as giants, elves, fairies, and talking animals. **Fairy tales** are a type of fantasy and are sometimes set in make-believe places. A fairy tale often begins with the familiar words, "Once upon a time."

Fables are like fantasy stories. For example, both fantasies and fables may contain talking animals. However, in a fantasy story, animals talk because they are special, or magical. In a fable, the animals think and talk like humans, but they behave like real-life animals.

Fables are usually short. There is a clear problem that is solved in the end. The author of a fable usually ends the story by telling the reader the lesson that he or she should learn from the story. Unlike fantasies, fables are almost always set in the real world.

Read the following examples of a fairy tale and a fable.

Fairy tale

It was getting late and the ball was ending. Cinderella had forgotten the time! She ran out the door in a hurry. As she raced down the steps, one of her glass slippers fell off.

The clock struck twelve. The beautiful coach that her fairy godmother had given her turned back into a pumpkin.

Fable

A wolf had a bone stuck in his throat. He went looking for someone to help him. "I would do anything for you if you would just take it out," he said. But everyone ran away. At last a crane agreed to help. It put its long neck down the wolf's throat and took the bone out. "Will you please give me my reward now?" asked the crane. The wolf said, "You should be happy. You put your head inside a wolf's mouth and took it out again! That reward is good enough."

Fantasies, fairy tales, and fables

◢ Use It

Look at the fairy tale on page 96 and answer the questions. Write your answers on the lines. Look at this example.

What magical event happens in this story?

<u>a coach becomes a pumpkin</u>

Now you try it.

1. Could the events in this story happen in the real world or in an imaginary world?

   _____

2. What unusual characters are in this story?

   _____

◢ Practice It

Read the fable on page 96. Then read the questions. Circle the letter of the correct answer.

1. **What is the setting of the fable?**

   A a magical planet

   B the real world

   C an island that floats on the water

   D a city in the clouds

2. **What is the lesson of this fable?**

   A Doing a good deed should be reward enough.

   B Do not chew your food too fast.

   C Do not put your head down a wolf's throat.

   D Do not do favors for wolves.

 Tip If the story has animal characters and teaches a lesson, it is probably a fable.

It's Hard to Believe

◧ Study It

Some stories about heroes are hard to believe. The heroes do things that seem impossible. These stories are called **legends.** Often, the hero in a legend reminds the reader of himself or herself. Legends teach us valuable lessons about ourselves.

Have you ever seen something you could not explain? Long ago, people did not know why the sun came up. They did not know what caused the seasons to change. **Myths** are stories that were created to explain such things. Myths gave people answers to their questions. They helped people make sense of the world. Myths often include gods as characters.

Read the following examples of a legend and a myth.

Legend

John Henry was a big, strong man. He could drive railroad spikes faster than any man.

One day, his boss wanted to decide whether to use machines or men to drive spikes. He asked John Henry to run a race. John Henry would have to drive spikes faster than a machine, which he did.

Myth

Long ago lived a dragon that could tear down trees. One day a girl from the Native American Spokane tribe was picking berries and saw the creature. It was sleeping on a hill where the Spokane River is today.

The girl ran quietly back to her village and told everyone what she had seen. The chief gathered his warriors and every rope in the village. Then the warriors crept up on the dragon. They tied it to several trees and then attacked it. The dragon woke up and instantly broke free. As he ran away, he tore a deep trench to Lake Coeur d'Alene in Idaho. The lake waters flowed through this trench, all the way to the sea. That is how the Spokane River was formed.

Myths/legends

Use It

Look at the legend on page 98. Then read the items. Write your answers on the lines. Look at this example.

Who is the hero of this story?

John Henry

Now you try it.

1. What is special about John Henry?

2. What did John Henry do in the race?

Practice It

Look at the myth on page 98. Then read the questions. Circle the letter of the correct answer.

1. **Which part of the story is NOT real?**

   A the Native American warriors

   B the Native American chief

   C the dragon

   D the Spokane River

2. **What does the myth explain?**

   A how the state of Idaho got its name

   B how the Spokane River was formed

   C how dragons came to be

   D how rope was first made

3. **What awoke the dragon?**

   A the girl picking berries

   B a tree falling

   C its own snoring

   D the attack by the warriors

Tip If the hero of a story does things that seem impossible, the story is probably a legend.

Stories Acted Out

◢ Study It

Plays are stories that are acted on a stage. Actors play the parts of the story's **characters.**

How do actors know what to say and do when they are on stage? What is the **setting,** or the place where the action occurs? People who write plays put that information into a **script.**

Scripts tell actors and readers the **dialogue,** or what characters say to one another. Scripts also have **stage directions** that tell what action is taking place and what the stage looks like.

Look at the script from *How the People Got Fire* by L. E. McCullough. The play is set in a forest, and the characters are the animals of the world. Notice the different parts.

Tag lines tell which character is speaking.

Stage directions describe the scene and tell what the characters are doing.

NARRATOR: And in awhile, all the animals of the World came: Frog . . . Fox . . . Snake . . . Wildcat . . . Mouse . . . Deer . . . Dog . . . Chipmunk . . . Skunk.

COYOTE: Animals of the World, we have seen smoke!

LIZARD: And where there is smoke —

LIZARD'S BROTHER: There is fire!

ANIMALS: *(cheer)* Hurrah! They have seen smoke! They have seen fire!

COYOTE: Quiet, please. This smoke and fire belongs to Thunder and Lightning.

ANIMALS: *(moans)* Oh, no . . . not Thunder and Lightning.

MOUSE: We must get this fire and bring it to The People.

FROG: That will not be easy. They say an evil bird, Woswosim, guards the fire at night. He never sleeps.

Lines tell what each character is saying.

Use It

Look at the play on the previous page. Then read the questions. Write your answers on the lines. Look at this example.

__a forest__   What is the setting of the play?

Now you try it.

_____ 1. Which character speaks first?

_____ 2. What do the characters do after the coyote mentions Thunder and Lighting?

Practice It

Read this scene from *Come Quick! A Play for April Fool's Day* by Sue Alexander. The scene takes place in a boy's room. The characters are a boy and his father. Then read the items. Circle the letter of the correct answer.

BOY: Father! PLEASE come quick! Now there is a seal in my room! And he is saying GWARK! And he is clapping his fins together — like this! (*The boy bounces like a seal and claps his hands.*) GWARK! GWARK!

FATHER: Hmmm. Maybe I had better go and look after all. If those animals ARE in your room, we will have to call the zoo! (*He puts down his book and gets up and goes out.*)

BOY: Ha! Ha! I did it! I made him look! And there's nothing there! What a good April Fool's joke!

1. **What do the stage directions tell you that the boy is doing?**

    A leaving the room

    B reading a book

    C bouncing a ball

    D acting like a seal

2. **What does the boy do in this play?**

    A He makes his father angry.

    B He tricks his father.

    C He makes his father laugh.

    D He protects his father.

> **Tip** Read the stage directions in a play to understand what the characters are feeling or doing.

Lesson 28

Musical Words

◣ Study It

Poems often describe the world around us or express feelings about a subject. **Poets,** or the writers of poems, usually use very few words and give them a musical sound.

Poetry uses all five senses: sight, sound, smell, taste, and touch. But sound and sight are used most often.

Look at the web to the right to see the ways that poets use these senses.

A poet arranges the sounds of words in a poem like a songwriter arranges notes in music. One type of sound used in poetry is **rhyme.** When the ends of words sound alike, they rhyme. In the line *Uncle Stan dropped the can,* the words Stan and can rhyme.

Like a piece of music, a poem has a beat. This is called **rhythm.** Rhythm helps create a mood. Notice how the words went, store, get, and more feel different than the other words when you read this line aloud: *I went to the store just to get a little more.*

The words in poetry also create **pictures** that you can see in your mind. Your imagination lets you see the valley in this line: *The bright sun cast its rays on the green valley.*

Read the poem "Deer," translated by Sylvia Cassedy and Parvathi Thampi.

> Beneath the harvest moon there trips
> a herd of prancing, spotted deer.
> Through the leafy woods they pass,
> searching for a field of grass;
> As dusk begins to disappear
> there come the dancing, spotted deer,
> with half a smile upon their lips.

The poem paints a playful picture of deer in the woods at night. The rhyming words trips and lips, pass and grass, and disappear and deer help present the scene. The rhythm suggests the movement of deer walking through the fields.

Poetry

This page may not be reproduced without permission of Steck-Vaughn.

Use It

Read the poem "The Sun Comes Up" by Carol Diggory Shields. Then answer the questions. Write your answers on the lines. Look at the example.

> The sun comes up, the moon goes down,
> By tick and tock a day goes round.
> The days go dancing, one by one,
> When seven pass, a week is done.
> The moon is counting in the sky,
> As week by week a month goes by.
> Month by month the seasons swing:
> Summer, autumn, winter, spring.
> The moon comes up, the sun goes down,
> And month by month a year goes round.

Which words in the poem rhyme? _____

_____

Now you try it.

1. What senses are used in the poem? _____

2. What word picture do you see? _____

_____

Practice It

Read the poem in the Use It section. Then answer the questions. Circle the letter of the correct answer.

1. **What is the poem about?**

   A a merry-go-round

   B sunshine

   C time

   D the planets

2. **What do the days do?**

   A go down

   B dance

   C come up

   D count

 Tip When you read a poem, look at and listen to the ways in which the poet uses words.

Unit 5
Test-Taking Strategy

Strategy: Read It Again

In this unit you learned about different kinds of books. Books can be fiction or nonfiction, poetry or stories. Knowing about different kinds of books will make answering test questions easier.

- Think about the information in the passage. Is the passage real or make-believe? Is it a play or a poem?
- Read the question and the answer choices. Reread the passage if you are not sure about the answer.

Try It Out

Read the story. Then answer the question. Circle the letter of the correct answer.

> Arthur was worried. The knight he served, Sir Kay, had left his sword back at the inn. Arthur had gone back to the inn to get the sword, but the inn was locked. He did not want to return without the sword. Arthur knew of a sword magically encased in a stone. He decided to get that sword. He found it easy to pull the sword out of the stone. He took the sword to Sir Kay.

This passage is an example of —

A an autobiography

B a poem

C a legend

D a play

Look at all of the answer choices. The passage is not an autobiography because Arthur did not write it himself. The passage does not have rhyming words or rhythm, so it is not a poem. Without dialogue or stage directions, the passage is not a play. Arthur was able to pull the sword from the stone, something that seemed to be impossible. Heroes in legends do things that seem impossible, so answer **C** is correct.

Unit 5 • Kinds of Books
Put It to the Test

This test will check what you have learned in this unit.

DIRECTIONS: Read each item. Circle the letter of the correct answer.

1. An interview is a good way to get information for —

   A a fiction book

   B a myth

   C a biography

   D an autobiography

2. Which of these has stage directions?

   A a biography

   B a play

   C a poem

   D a fable

3. Which of these uses rhythm and rhyme?

   A a biography

   B a myth

   C a fantasy

   D a poem

4. In what kind of book do gods often appear?

   A myths

   B nonfiction

   C fables

   D plays

5. Which of these has make-believe people or events?

   A autobiography

   B nonfiction

   C fiction

   D biography

6. Who is the main character in a legend?

   A an animal

   B a god

   C a hero

   D an actor

7. An author would have to know facts about something in order to write —

   A a poem

   B a legend

   C a short story

   D an informational text

GO ON

Achieve It! Practice Cards

_____

8. **Which of these is an example of fiction?**

   A a biography

   B a fantasy

   C an informational text

   D an autobiography

9. **Which of these books is MOST likely to have such characters as elves and giants?**

   A a biography

   B a fairy tale

   C a legend

   D a myth

10. **To learn about tigers, the book that would be the MOST helpful is —**

    A *The Big Book of Animals*

    B *All About Tigers*

    C *Tiger Finds a Toy*

    D *Jungle Adventures*

11. **In which type of story is an author MOST likely to teach a lesson?**

    A a myth

    B a legend

    C a fantasy

    D a fable

12. **In which kind of book does the author write about his or her own life?**

    A an informational text

    B a fiction story

    C an autobiography

    D a biography

13. **Some myths are written to —**

    A express feelings

    B teach a lesson

    C get people to do something

    D explain something in nature

14. **Which of these describes nonfiction?**

    A It comes from the writer's imagination.

    B It contains facts, but some things are make-believe.

    C It is about real people or things.

    D It has make-believe settings.

15. **The lines in a play —**

    A tell how the stage looks

    B are the words the actors speak

    C are the characters

    D tell the actor what to do

Achieve It! Practice Cards

Understanding Parts of a Story

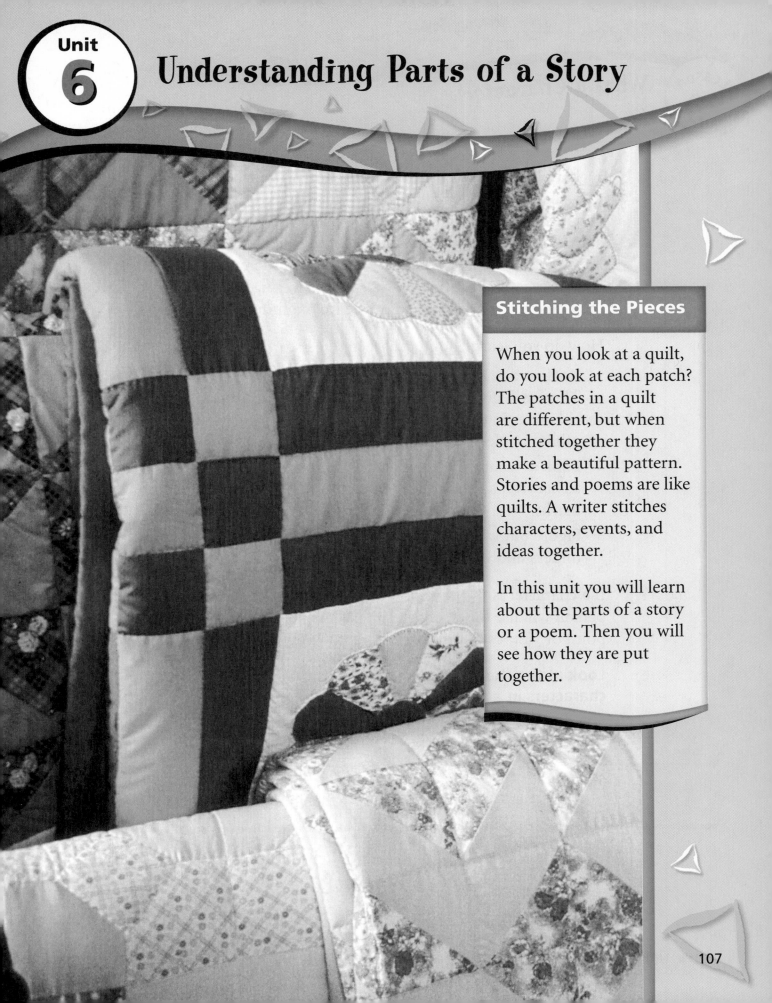

Stitching the Pieces

When you look at a quilt, do you look at each patch? The patches in a quilt are different, but when stitched together they make a beautiful pattern. Stories and poems are like quilts. A writer stitches characters, events, and ideas together.

In this unit you will learn about the parts of a story or a poem. Then you will see how they are put together.

What a Character!

Study It

A **character** is an imaginary person, animal, or make-believe creature in a story. Even though characters are imaginary, you often learn about them in the same ways that you learn about real people. As events happen in the story, the writer may tell you what characters look like. You will see what they do and say. Many writers also let you see what a character is thinking and feeling. Most writers make their characters seem like someone we might meet in real life.

How do you learn about a character in a story?

- Look at descriptions of what the character looks like and does. These will give you clues about what has happened to the character in the past and how he or she wants to be seen by other people.

- Look at what the character says, thinks, and feels. In a story, a character's words and thoughts usually appear in quotation marks.

- Figure out what the character needs or wants to help you understand why he or she acts in a certain way.

If a character is the **narrator,** or the person telling the story, that person will use the words I or me to tell the story. The narrator's point of view can also help you get to know him or her.

Look at the chart. It shows questions that you should ask about characters in a story.

What does the character look like and do?	What does the character say, think, or feel?	What does the character need or want?

Character/speaker

Read the story.

Tyler was late for school again. He had forgotten to set his alarm clock. "Rats! I slept late again!" he yelled when he woke up.

Tyler jumped out of bed and pulled on the clothes he wore yesterday. His shirt was inside out, and his jeans had muddy knees. Tyler didn't care. He picked up a pair of smelly socks and ran downstairs.

"Late again! I'm in trouble," thought Tyler as he poured cereal into a bowl. "Dad, I need a ride to school!" Tyler called. Then he saw the note on the table. It said, "Enjoy the first day of summer. Love, Dad." Tyler dropped his spoon in surprise. "Never mind!" he said to himself.

Look at the chart. It shows how the questions about the character can be answered.

What does the character look like and do?	What does the character say, think, or feel?	What does the character need or want?
He wakes up late.	He says, "Rats! I slept late again."	He wants to keep from getting into trouble.
He pulls on dirty clothes, and he looks sloppy.	He thinks, "Late again! I'm in trouble."	He wants a ride to school.
He makes breakfast.	He feels worried, and then surprised and happy.	
He tries to ask his dad for a ride.		
He finds a note.		
He drops his spoon in surprise.		

What kind of person is Tyler? He seems to be forgetful and messy. Notice the sentence "Tyler was late for school again." The word <u>again</u> is a clue that he has slept late before.

Use It

Read the story. Look for clues that help you answer questions about Nina's character. Then write your answers on the lines. Look at the example.

Nina sat at the piano with her hands in her lap. "I don't want to practice today," she thought.

Nina stared out the window. She could see her sister playing kickball with her friends. "I want to go outside," Nina said to her mother.

Nina's mother closed the curtain. "If you practice for half an hour, then you can go out, okay?" she said.

Nina thought her mother's idea was fair and started to play.

What does Nina look like at the beginning of the story?
She is sitting with her hands on her lap.

Now you try it.

1. What feelings does Nina express in the story?

   _____

2. What does Nina want to do?

   _____

3. What makes you think that Nina is willing to listen to her mother?

   _____

   _____

Practice It

Read this passage from the book *Stellaluna* by Janell Cannon. Then read each item. Circle the letter of the correct answer.

As the birds flew among the bats, Flap said, "I feel upside down here."

So the birds hung by their feet.

"Wait until dark," Stellaluna said excitedly. "We will fly at night."

When night came Stellaluna flew away. Pip, Flitter, and Flap leapt from the tree to follow her.

"I can't see a thing!" yelled Pip.

"Neither can I," howled Flitter.

"Aaeee!" shrieked Flap.

"They're going to crash," gasped Stellaluna. "I must rescue them!"

Stellaluna swooped about, grabbing her friends in the air. She lifted them to a tree, and the birds grasped a branch. Stellaluna hung from the limb above them.

1. **Why did Pip, Flitter, and Flap decide to hang by their feet?**

   A Their feathers were dirty, and they wanted to shake them out.

   B They wanted to do the same thing as Stellaluna did.

   C Their wings were tired, so they were resting.

   D They wanted to exercise their legs.

2. **How did Stellaluna feel when the birds nearly crashed in the dark?**

   A She did not really care.

   B She was sad because she could not help them.

   C She was worried and knew she had to help them.

   D She was happy because it would help them learn to fly at night.

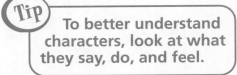

Tip
To better understand characters, look at what they say, do, and feel.

Then What Happened?

Study It

A story has a setting, characters, and a **plot.** The plot usually contains a **conflict,** or a problem that must be solved. Sometimes there is more than one conflict. The plot makes the story interesting because we want to continue reading to find out what happens. The plot also contains a **resolution,** or **solution,** or the way that the problem is solved. To understand the plot of a story, ask yourself these questions.

- What problem does the main character have?
- What does the character do to solve the problem?
- What is the result of the character's action?

The author usually identifies a problem near the beginning of the story.

Read the beginning of this story.

> Chris was a very good speller. She always got all the spelling words right. Her best friend Andy thought that she should be in the state spelling contest. But Chris was too shy. So Andy sent her name to the contest without telling Chris.

Look at the chart. It shows the beginning of the story's plot.

Who are the characters?	What is the problem?	What happens?
Chris and Andy	Chris is good at spelling, but she is shy.	Andy enters Chris in a spelling contest without telling her.

In the beginning of the story, you meet the characters, Chris and Andy. You learn that Chris is shy. Then you find out about the first event in the story when Andy enters Chris in a spelling contest but does not tell her.

Can you predict, or guess, what might happen next?

Plot

Read the middle of the story.

Chris felt mad. She said, "I won't do it."

Andy said, "I will help you get ready." They practiced spelling every day.

Chris went to the contest, but she was still afraid. Andy said, "Just pretend you are practicing with me."

Chris did her best. Soon there was only one other speller on the stage. He misspelled a word. Now it was Chris's turn. She closed her eyes, took a deep breath, and spelled the word.

Look at the chart. It shows how the plot continues.

What is the problem?	What solution is offered?	What is the result?
Chris says she will not go to the contest.	Andy helps Chris get ready.	Chris goes to the contest and is one of the two final spellers.

Can you predict what will happen next? Notice how the plot of the story holds the reader's interest. Does Chris spell the word correctly and win the contest?

Read the ending of the story.

Chris opened her eyes. Everyone was cheering. Someone gave her a gold statue. People took her picture. Andy ran up and exclaimed, "You won!"

Look at the chart. It shows how the problem in the plot is solved.

What happens?	What happens next?	What is the final result?
Chris opens her eyes and sees people cheering.	People take her picture and give her a statue.	Chris finds out she has won the contest.

Many stories are longer than this one, but the plot of a story usually follows the same pattern. The main character has one or more problems. The story reaches its high point when the problem is most difficult. The story usually ends when the problem is solved.

Use It

Read the story. Then fill in the missing information in the chart.

Mario thought hospitals were scary and did not want to visit his grandmother there. But his sister Abby made him go. The hospital had many hallways. Mario stopped to tie his shoe. When he stood up, Abby was gone. Mario was lost!

Problem #1	Problem #2	Problem #3	Problem #4
Mario did not want to go to the hospital because he was scared.	Mario's sister made him go to the hospital.	Mario stopped to tie his shoe.	Mario lost track of his sister, and he got lost.

Now you try it.

Mario saw a nurse at a desk and told her, "I'm lost."

The woman looked up his grandmother's room number and walked Mario to the room. His grandmother and Abby were happy to see Mario.

"What happened to you?" they asked.

"Nothing. I just stopped to talk to one of my friends here at the hospital," Mario said, giving the nurse a secret smile.

What is the problem?	What solution is offered?	What is the result?
_____	_____	_____
	_____	_____
		_____

Practice It

Read the passage from "Oh No, It's Robert: Pink Underwear" by Barbara Seuling. Then answer the questions. Circle the letter of the correct answer.

Inventions Day was here at last. Robert was ready. Mrs. Bernthal asked for the first volunteer. Susanne Lee Rodgers waved her hand and then went up to the front of the room. She carried a small lamp. Mrs. Bernthal plugged the lamp into a wall socket.

Susanne Lee wrote THE ELECTRIC LIGHT on the blackboard. She clicked on the lamp.

"We use electric lights every day," she began. Susanne Lee must have read forty books on Thomas Edison and the electric light bulb for her report. By the time she was finished, Robert felt as though he had read forty books, too.

1. **How did Robert probably feel about Inventions Day?**

   A He was unhappy that Inventions Day was here.

   B He was worried about Inventions Day.

   C He was looking forward to Inventions Day.

   D He was sad because he wasn't interested in inventions.

2. **How did Robert feel about Susanne Lee's report?**

   A He wished that he had chosen Thomas Edison for his report.

   B He thought her report was too long.

   C He was happy that he had not volunteered to give his report.

   D He thought Susanne Lee's report was very interesting.

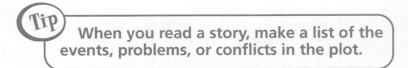
Tip When you read a story, make a list of the events, problems, or conflicts in the plot.

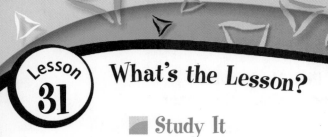

What's the Lesson?

Study It

A **theme** is an idea that a writer wants to share. A story's theme tells you something important about life. It is like a lesson.

The theme of a story is not the topic. The topic of a story might be about a boy who loses a bicycle. The theme might be that losing something can teach us to care more about people than things. A writer does not need to say the theme of a story in the story itself.

To find the theme, use clues from the story.

- Look at what the speaker or narrator says. The theme is sometimes an important idea that the speaker or narrator talks about at the end of a story.

- Look at what the characters say and do. Characters often suggest the theme of the story when they talk to other characters.

- Notice what the characters learn. The theme is often an important idea that a character learns.

Read the passage.

My grandmother filled little pots with dirt and put a seed in each one. Each day she talked to the pots. I asked my grandmother why she talked to the dirt. She said, "Anna, I am not talking to dirt. I am talking to the plants. Even though I can't see them, I know they are growing." Grandmother knows that you must believe in things even if you can't see them.

Look at the chart. It shows how clues can help you find the theme.

What is the passage about?	What Is the theme?	What clues told you the theme?
A grandmother who plants seeds	Sometimes you must believe in things even if you can't see them.	Anna's grandmother talks to plants she can't see. Grandmother knows the plants are growing even if she can't see them.

Theme

Both characters talk about the important idea that you can believe in something even if you can't see it.

Read the passage.

Nick wanted a basketball for his birthday. He told everyone, "I sure hope I get a basketball." Ten of Nick's friends came to his birthday party. Each one gave him a basketball.

"Gosh! I wanted one basketball, not ten!" said Nick.

His dad said, "You should be careful what you wish for. Your wish might come true."

Look at the chart. It shows how clues can help you find the theme.

What is the passage about?	What is the theme?	What clues told you the theme?
A boy who wants a basketball for his birthday	Wishing for something may not bring you what you want.	Nick was not happy when he got ten basketballs. Nick's dad told him to be careful about his wishes.

To find the theme, look at what the characters say. Then think about what the characters learn at the end of the story.

◢ **Use It**

Read the story. Look for clues that tell you the theme. Then answer the questions. Look at the example.

Jen felt sad because her best friend was moving away. Jen and Sarah had been friends since preschool. They saw each other every day. Sometimes they talked on the phone at night, too.

Jen's mother said, "You can still be friends even when you and Sarah are far away. I still talk to my best friend from when I was your age."

Jen did not believe her mother. She stayed in her room on the day Sarah moved away. At dinner, she said, "I will never talk to my best friend again."

Then the phone rang. It was Sarah. They talked a long time. Later Jen said, "I think maybe you were right, Mom. Sarah and I will stay friends forever."

What is the story about?

a girl who is sad because her friend has moved away

Now you try it.

1. What is the theme of this story?

   _____

2. What is one clue that helps tell you the theme of this story?

   _____
   _____
   _____
   _____
   _____

◢ Practice It

Read the story. Then read each question. Circle the letter of the correct answer.

The Harris family gathering was taking place in Janelle's backyard. "This family gathering is great," Janelle said to her Aunt Liz.

"That's nice," Aunt Liz sighed. "I'm glad you are having fun. These gatherings are a lot of work. I never seem to have any fun at them."

Janelle came up with an idea to make the day special for her aunt. She and her cousin Whitney began asking each person in the crowd a question about Aunt Liz.

After lunch, Janelle stood up. "Listen, everyone. Whitney and I put together this book. It's called <u>Why We Love Aunt Liz</u>. The girls took turns reading. When they finished, everyone stood up and cheered.

"Thank you, girls," Aunt Liz said. "I am really glad I came."

1. **What is the story about?**

   A good food to make at a family gathering

   B how to put a book together

   C a girl and her cousin who make a book of nice stories about their aunt

   D a special birthday party

2. **What is the theme of this story?**

   A Family gatherings are a lot of fun.

   B Even if you think your hard work goes unnoticed, people appreciate it.

   C If you work hard, people will write nice things about you.

   D It is hard to make a book.

 Tip To find the theme, think about what the characters learn from what happened in the story.

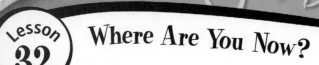

Where Are You Now?

◢ Study It

The **setting** of a story tells you where a story took place and when it happened. Sometimes writers tell you about the setting directly. At other times, they only give you clues. They talk about how the setting looks, sounds, smells, and feels.

A story's setting

- tells you the **place** where the story happens (in a kitchen, on a boat, in the woods, at a bus stop)
- tells you the **time** when the story happens (100 years ago, yesterday morning, in the year 1945)

Details about a setting can help give the story a certain **mood,** or feeling. Two stories with the same setting, but different details, can give you different feelings. Think of a story about walking in the woods. One writer might say that the light shines through the leaves like stars in the sky. Another writer might say that the branches are so tangled that no light can shine through. The mood of the first setting is pleasant. The mood of the second setting is gloomy.

Read the passage.

Robbie walked alone through a field, the snow crunching under his boots. The wind shook the trees. The pond, covered with a thin sheet of ice, was still.

Look at the chart. It answers questions about where the story happened.

Setting	
Where does the story happen?	**What clues help you?**
in a field	Robbie walked through an empty field.
in the snow	The snow crunched.
near trees	The trees shook.
near a pond	A thin sheet of ice covered the pond.

Setting

Read the next passage. Then look at the chart. It answers questions about when the story happened.

The sky was dark even though it was only 4:30 P.M. Robbie had stayed late at school to practice basketball. As he kicked the snow, he thought, "It never gets this cold before Thanksgiving."

Setting	
When does the story happen?	**What clues help you?**
in late afternoon	It was only 4:30 P.M.
on a school day	Robbie had stayed late at school.
in November	It never gets this cold before Thanksgiving.

Read this passage.

The houses next to the field were dark. Shadows in the snow made everything seem a little strange. Robbie thought, "Did I take the wrong path by mistake?" He started to walk faster through the snow.

Look at the chart. It will give you clues about the mood of the story.

Mood	
How does the story makes you feel?	**What clues help you?**
a little scared	the dark houses
worried	the snow's strange appearance
	Robbie's fear of being lost

Read the story. Then answer the questions about the setting. Look at the example.

The kitchen of the farmhouse was large and warm. The morning sun poured through the window onto the wooden floor. A fire was burning in the stove. The smell of the baking bread filled the air.

The clock struck six o'clock. The old woman stopped sewing and put a clean apron over her long skirts. Today was Saturday. She wanted her son to drive the wagon into town and take her to buy some supplies.

Where did the story happen?
in the kitchen of a farmhouse

Now you try it.

1. Which sentence in the story tells you where the story takes place?

   _____

2. How did the setting of the story make you feel?

   _____

3. When does the story take place?

   _____

   _____

4. Which sentences in the story tell you when the story takes place?

   _____

   _____

   _____

   _____

◼ Practice It

Read the passage. Then read the items. Circle the letter of the correct answer.

The room was small but very clean. It smelled like soap. There were two beds. Each bed had a blue blanket and a white pillow. The orange curtains blocked out the hot summer sun.

I put my bags down on the floor and sat on the bed. We had been driving all day and were tired. Dad said, "Do you want to eat dinner now or go for a swim?" I was hungry, but the hotel pool would close at dark. "We should go swimming first," I said.

1. **Where did the story happen?**

   A in a car

   B in a swimming pool

   C in a hotel room

   D in a hospital room

2. **When did the story take place?**

   A on a summer evening

   B on a winter morning

   C on a spring night

   D on an autumn day

3. **Which words tell you when the story takes place?**

   A small but very clean

   B two beds

   C on the floor and on the bed

   D the hot summer sun

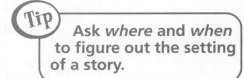

Tip Ask *where* and *when* to figure out the setting of a story.

What's It Like?

▰ Study It

Figures of speech make writing more lively and interesting. They show new or different ways of describing or comparing things. Many popular sayings are figures of speech.

- A **simile** (sim´-ə-lē´) shows how two unlike things can seem alike. A simile always uses the words <u>as</u> or <u>like</u> to compare.
- A **metaphor** (met´-ə-fôr´) shows how two unlike things can seem alike. A metaphor does not use <u>as</u> or <u>like</u>.
- **Personification** means treating an object or animal like a person.
- **Hyperbole** (hi-pur´-bə-lē) means overstating a fact or opinion. Hyperboles are often meant to be funny.

Look at these figures of speech.

Similes   **My pancakes were as tough <u>as</u> tires. They tasted <u>like</u> cardboard.**

The similes above use <u>as</u> and <u>like</u> to show how the pancakes felt and tasted. Pancakes are not really like tires or cardboard. The similes show that the pancakes were hard to chew and tasteless.

Metaphors   **The baby was a little doll. She was a perfect picture.**

The metaphors compare the baby to a doll and a picture, without using the words <u>like</u> or <u>as</u>.

Personification   **The sun pushed its yellow face through the clouds.**

The sun does not really have a face. The writer is using personification.

Hyperbole   **Today was the longest day of Tina's life. It was 100 hours long.**

The hyperbole makes it sound as if this day were longer than other days. In real life, all days are 24 hours long. But this figure of speech makes you feel how the day felt to Tina.

   Figurative language

Read the poem.

Ode to a Coconut

In the palm-tree throne,
so close to the sun,
you sit, like king of the tropical nuts.

A whole world in yourself,
covered in tall brown grass,
with your milky ocean protected inside.

In the warm salty breeze
of a forgotten kingdom,
you quietly soak up the view.

Waiting for the moment
when the wind's steady push
knocks you back to earth where you
started.

Your crown on the ground,
Oh hard king,
is now in the hands of whoever comes first.

Maybe an ocean wave
scoops you up in its arms,
and takes you off home.

Or maybe just silence
and sun and time
will let you sit and sprout a new throne.

Held up to the sky,
young ones will grow
and take over your seat in the sun.

Look at the chart. It shows figures of speech from the poem.

Figure of Speech	Example from the Poem
Metaphor	"In the palm-tree throne" compares the tree to a throne, but does not use the words <u>like</u> or <u>as</u>.
Simile	The phrase "like king of the tropical nuts" compares the coconut to a king using the word <u>like</u>.
Personification	The words "you quietly soak up the view" treat the coconut like a human. A coconut cannot have a view because coconuts cannot see.
Hyperbole	"A whole world in yourself" is an exaggeration because a coconut cannot be as large as the whole world.

◢ Use It

Look at the passage. Identify each underlined figure of speech. Some figures of speech will be found more than once. Write your answers on the lines. Look at the examples.

David woke up with a cold. He felt awful. His head felt as heavy as a bowling ball. His throat was sore. His nose was a dripping faucet. His mother put her hand on his forehead. She said, "You are on fire! Go back to bed and get some rest." David went back to bed. Sleep soon took him in its arms. He woke up the next morning, looking like a blooming flower. When he walked outside, the sun kissed his cheeks.

| simile | metaphor | personification | hyperbole |

_____simile_____ 1. His head felt as heavy as a bowling ball.

_____metaphor_____ 2. His nose was a dripping faucet.

Now you try it.

_____ 1. You are on fire!

_____ 2. Sleep soon took him in its arms.

_____ 3. looking like a blooming flower

_____ 4. the sun kissed his cheeks

Practice It

Read the poem. Then read the items. Circle the letter of the correct answer.

Look at that!
Look at that!
But when you look
there's no cat.

Without a purr
just a flash of fur
and gone
like a ghost.

The most
you see
are two tiny
green traffic lights
staring at the night.

1. **Which of the following choices is a simile?**

   A just a flash of fur

   B like a ghost

   C two tiny green traffic lights

   D without a purr

2. **The "two tiny green traffic lights" in the poem are really —**

   A a porch light

   B the cat's fur

   C the cat's eyes

   D a ghost

 To find a simile, look for a comparison using <u>like</u> or <u>as</u>.

How Writing Comes to Life

◼ Study It

Poets and other writers choose words carefully. They use words to fill your mind with pictures, feelings, and thoughts. Storytellers and poets use language to help you share and enjoy the writer's experiences.

- **Words that touch your senses** Sense words make you think about seeing, hearing, touching, tasting, and smelling what the author is writing about. Notice the sense words in these sentences. "The old beach house smelled of salt and fish. The sand crunched under our shoes."

- **Words that rhyme** Words that rhyme end with the same vowel sounds and consonants sounds. How, now, and cow are words that rhyme.

- **Words that have rhythm** Rhythm is the way words are stressed when you read them aloud. Writers place words in certain ways so that they have a beat in much the same way that music does.

- **Words with special sounds** The way words sound also makes them musical. **Alliteration** is similar to rhyme. It happens when writers use words that start with the same letter or consonant sound, such as "Peg punched the pink pillow." **Assonance** is another kind of sound similar to rhyme. The words contain similar vowel sounds but do not rhyme. "Sadie waved her faded daisy" is an example of assonance.

Read the poem.

The rain played in the yard all day.

It jumped into puddles, and it danced on the grass.

It drummed against the windows and it pounded
   on the glass.

It fell down the drainpipe after running off the roof.

I think that rain is silly. Now I've got lots of proof.

Poetic language

Look at the chart to see how the writer uses language.

Sense words (Seeing, Hearing, Feeling, Tasting, Smelling)	**Seeing:** The rain jumped, danced, fell, and ran. **Hearing:** It drummed against windows and pounded on the glass.
Rhyme	glass and grass roof and proof
Rhythm	The rhythm is quick, like rain falling.
Alliteration	running, roof down the drain pipe
Assonance	rain, played, day jumped, puddles danced, grass

Language is also an important part of stories.

Read the passage.

The summer sunlight slipped silently into Danny's bedroom and sat for a moment on his pillow. Then it wandered lightly across his forehead and along his eyelashes. Danny woke up slowly, his eyes still closed, and stretched lazily. Each of his senses tuned in to the new day. He heard the first chirping of bird songs and breathed in the warm smell of pancakes cooking on the griddle downstairs. Then his eyes popped open. He threw the covers back in one quick move and bounced out of bed. This was the first day of summer vacation! He didn't want to miss a minute of it!

Look at the chart to see how the writer uses language.

Sense words (Seeing, Hearing, Touching Tasting, Smelling)	**Seeing:** sunlight slips into the room **Touching:** stretching lazily, throwing back the covers **Hearing:** chirping birds **Smelling:** pancakes
Rhyme	The passage does not have rhyme.
Rhythm	slow in the first part of the passage; quick in second part
Alliteration	summer, sunlight; slipped silently
Assonance	woke, slowly, closed

Use It

Read the poem. Look at the language the poet uses.

The winter wind blows so fierce and so cold.
It bites like a bear that is cranky and old.
I wear coat and boots. I wear mittens and hat,
But still the wind howls like a mean alley cat.
It turns my nose red and my ten fingers blue.
The cold has us cornered. What can we do?
Except wait for spring when wind becomes nice.
Until then keep warm! And don't slip on the ice!

Fill in the missing information.

Sense words (Seeing, Hearing, Touching Tasting, Smelling)	**Seeing:** red nose, blue fingers **Hearing:** _____ **Touching:** _____ _____
Rhyme	cold/old _____ _____ _____
Rhythm	The rhythm is playful, like the poem.
Alliteration	winter wind _____ _____ _____
Assonance	spring, wind

Practice It

Read the passage. Then read the questions. Circle the letter of the correct answer.

"Let's go to the lighthouse," I said to my dad. We walked near the waves and watched the water. The storm had turned the ocean from a bright blue to a dark gray. Now the sea looked like dirty mop water. Each wave hit the beach with a crash. The water roared and hissed as the waves slid back into the sea. The air was full of salt and circling birds. The sand was as flat and cold as a ski trail.

1. **Which words from the passage make you think about how things look?**

   A   walked near the waves

   B   the sea looked like dirty mop water

   C   hit the beach with a crash

   D   go to the lighthouse

2. **Which words use alliteration?**

   A   hit the beach with a crash

   B   full of salt and circling birds

   C   flat and cold as a ski trail

   D   walked near the waves and watched the water

3. **Which words make you think about how something feels to the touch?**

   A   from a bright blue to a dark gray

   B   hit the beach with a crash

   C   roared and hissed

   D   flat and cold as a ski trail

Tip
As you read, see how the writer uses words that appeal to your senses.

Behind the Scenes

◼ Study It

Stories are like windows that let you look into different places and times. When you read, you can learn about many kinds of people and their ways of living. Writers give you clues about their characters' worlds and themselves. As you read, ask yourself these questions.

- What are the characters' names and what languages do they speak?
- What traditions do they have?
- What do you know about the author's background?
- What ideas are important to the writer?

Read the passage from *Song of the Honda* by Rector Lawrence Lee.

> Finally it was completed, and all three were hot and tired. Tomo ran to the end of the patio to get a good look at the finished oven.
>
> "Hola!" he shouted with pride. "You can see it a long way off."
>
> "A little lopsided," his father declared, "but it's not too bad."
>
> "Maybe it will fall down when it gets hot," said Juan. "Then we won't have to poke it with poles."

Look at the chart to find clues about the characters' world.

Clues About the Character's World	Your Conclusions
• The boys' names are Tomo and Juan. • Tomo speaks Spanish and English. • The boys and their father have built an oven.	The story may be about a Spanish-speaking family that lives in the United States. The family may be from long ago, or they may be practicing an old tradition of oven building. The writer may be a Spanish speaker who thinks family activities are important.

You can use the clues to get ideas about the characters and the writer. Writers often write about the world they know or remember.

Cultural/historical influences

Read the passage.

The first thing my sister Nuala and I loved about America was the food. At home in Ireland, my father's potato plants caught a plant disease. We had little to eat, and life was hard. So we moved to America.

Near the place where our boat landed in America, the city streets were filled with people and horses. We did not go far before we saw the shops. Our mouths watered when we saw the baskets of food. Nuala said, "Oh, look! Apples!"

Look at the chart. It shows clues from the passage and the conclusions you can make.

Clues About the Characters' World	Your Conclusions
• The sister's name is Nuala. • The character's home was in Ireland. • The characters took a boat to America. • The city streets are filled with people and horses. • The children are excited to see food.	The characters are new to America from Ireland. The characters must be from long ago because there are horses in the street, and they came to the United States by boat. The writer must know about life for Irish people in the United States. He or she may be writing about a true life event.

To learn about the world of the characters and the writer, look for the characters' names and how they speak, and clues about how and when the characters live. Then look for clues about the writer's life or ideas.

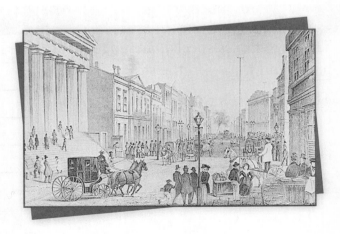

Use It

Read the passage. Look for clues that tell you about the characters and the writer.

Four times a week Lilikala went to the halau, or school. There she learned about the hula, the dance that is special to the people of Hawaii. Just like her mother and grandmother, Lilikala was learning the songs and dances of the islands.

At first, Lilikala was not sure she wanted to go to the halau. She would miss playing computer games with her friends. Then her grandmother said, "Lili, the hula is more than a dance. It tells our history as a people. It shows how much we love the land."

What conclusions can you draw about the characters' world? Write your answers in the chart.

Clues About the Characters' World	Your Conclusions
• Lilikala is from Hawaii. • She is going to a special school. • She likes to play computer games. • The hula and the halau are part of Lilikala's family history.	_____ _____ _____

What conclusions can you draw about the writer? Write your answers in the chart.

Clues About the Writer	Your Conclusions
• The writer uses special language—halau and hula—in the story. • The writer tells what the hula means.	_____ _____ _____ _____ _____

Practice It

Read the story. Then read the items. Circle the letter of the correct answer.

Aunt Lula Mae sat in a rocking chair on her front porch. She took a drink of iced tea. She said, "Did you finish your homework?"

"Yes," I said.

"Yes, *ma'am*," she said to correct me. "In my day, young people were polite. And Southern girls did not wear blue jeans. They dressed like ladies."

"Things are different today. I can wear jeans, and I can be anything I want. Like a doctor."

Aunt Lula Mae said, "Fine. Be a woman doctor. But you should still be polite."

"Yes, ma'am," I said.

1. **What would be the BEST conclusion to make about the characters in this story?**

   A The speaker and her aunt both think that girls today should wear blue jeans.

   B The speaker and her aunt both want her to become a doctor.

   C The speaker and her aunt both think girls should wear dresses.

   D The speaker and her aunt have different ideas about how young people today should act.

2. **From reading the story, you can tell that the writer probably thinks that it is important to —**

   A become a doctor

   B be polite

   C wear blue jeans

   D drink iced tea

Tip When you read, look for clues in the story that tell about the character's life and the writer's ideas.

Unit 6
Test-Taking Strategy

Strategy: Find the Parts

In this unit you learned that a story has characters, a plot, a setting, and a theme. Finding these parts can help you answer questions about a story on a test.

- As you read, look for clues that help answer these questions.
  Who are the characters?
  What is happening?
  Where and when is the story happening?

- Look for language that helps you picture the story in your mind.

- After you finish reading, ask yourself *What did the character learn?* and *What did I learn as a reader?* These questions help you find the theme of the story.

Try It Out
Read the passage. Then answer the question.

> The cold air bit at Ben's fingers. He unhooked the dogs from the sled. After Ben fed them, the dogs dug holes in the snow for sleeping. Ben sat by the fire and studied the stars in the black sky. They helped guide him on his journey.

Which words tell you that the story probably takes place in Alaska?

A   sat by the fire

B   cold air bit at Ben's fingers

C   studied the stars in the black sky

D   unhooked the dogs from the sled

The story gives lots of clues that Ben is in a cold place. The air bites at his fingers. Ben sits by a fire. But winter weather happens in many places. The best clue is that Ben unhooks the dogs from the sled. Dog sleds are common in Alaska. So the answer is **D.**

Unit 6 • Understanding Parts of a Story
Put It to the Test

This test will check what you have learned in this unit.

DIRECTIONS: Read the story. Then read each item. Circle the letter of the correct answer.

Summer Camp Lesson

It was Max's first time at summer camp. He was excited but also a little worried. He was small for his age. He was afraid that he would not make any friends.

A woman named Jenny took Max to his tent. He would share it with two other boys. "Your tent team is called the Yellow Jackets," said Jenny. Max looked at the other boys. They were not wearing jackets. "Where are your yellow jackets?" asked Max.

"Yellow jackets are like bees. They are insects that sting," said Tyler, who was a big kid with freckles. He sounded a little mean.

"Yes, but real yellow jackets do not sting each other," said Alec. Max felt worried. He tried not to show it. "Tyler is okay," Alec whispered to Max. "You just need to get used to him. I did. Trust me."

Max enjoyed life at camp. But he stayed out of Tyler's way. Tyler called him "Shorty" and would say things like "Get out of my way, or I'll step on you."

One day Tyler lost his watch. It had fallen between some rocks by the pond. Tyler's hand was too big to reach it. He said, "Hey, Shorty. Can you get my watch?" Max thought it was a trick. The hot sun pressed down on him. He started to sweat. But he decided to trust Tyler. He reached down and grabbed the watch like a fresh peach from a tree. Tyler said, "Thanks a lot! You're okay, Shorty!"

Max took a deep breath and said, "You're welcome. But could you please call me Max?" Tyler said, "You got it, Max."

GO ON

1. **At the start of the story, Max wants to —**

   A stay out of Tyler's way

   B go home

   C make friends

   D trust Tyler

2. **Which word best describes the character of Max at the beginning of the story?**

   A brave

   B worried

   C silly

   D friendly

3. **What is the first thing that happens to Max?**

   A He meets Tyler and Alec.

   B He stays out of Tyler's way.

   C He picks up Tyler's watch.

   D He goes to his tent.

4. **The story takes place —**

   A at summer school

   B at summer camp

   C in Max's neighborhood

   D in winter

5. **What idea does Alec talk about with Max?**

   A being afraid

   B feeling different

   C trusting others

   D acting brave

6. **What word best describes Max at the end of the story?**

   A sad

   B trusting

   C afraid

   D angry

7. **When Tyler asks Max for help, Max decides to —**

   A trust Tyler

   B stay out of Tyler's way

   C ask Alec for help

   D share a peach with Tyler

GO ON

Achieve It! Practice Cards

8. **What important idea does Max learn in the story?**

   A   Summer camp is fun.

   B   Tyler is okay.

   C   It is good to have small hands.

   D   It is all right to trust people.

9. **Which words from the story show a thing acting like a person?**

   A   insects that sting

   B   fallen between some rocks

   C   hot sun pressed down on him

   D   like a fresh peach from a tree

10. **Which words from the story compare unlike things?**

    A   small for his age

    B   too big to reach it

    C   like a fresh peach from a tree

    D   big kid with freckles

11. **Read this passage.**

    > The sun set slowly over the green fields. A light breeze whistled softly through the trees. Soon it would be dark.

    Which group of words all start with the same sound?

    A   sun, set, slowly

    B   green, breeze, trees

    C   through, the, trees

    D   green, light, dark

12. **Read the poem.**

    > We three sisters climbed the tree.
    > We felt like birds, and as free.
    > We let our imaginations fly
    > To sail out over the sea.

    Which words from the poem rhyme?

    A   tree, free, sea

    B   the, sea, let

    C   sisters, sail, sea

    D   our, out, over

13. **Read the passage.**

    > Dear Teddy,
    >   This letter may not reach you soon. I sent it by Pony Express. But it takes a long time for the ponies to cross the mountains. Soon the train will come to our town.

    The passage was probably written —

    A   by a woman

    B   a long time ago

    C   last week

    D   by a young person

GO ON

Achieve It! Practice Cards

14. Read the passage.

> Back when I was young, we walked to school. We did not have school buses like you kids have today.

The passage was probably written —

A a long time ago

(B) by a young person

C by an older person

D by a woman

15. Read the passage.

> I learned a lot that summer. Mostly, I learned that Mr. Wiggins was not nearly as rude and grumpy as we boys thought he was. Once I got to know him, I saw how kind he was to the stray animals he cared for. I guess people need to look a little deeper before they make up their minds about someone.

The writer probably wrote this in a story to show —

A plot

B setting

(C) mood

D theme

16. Read the passage.

> The fog wound around the bare branches of the trees. Shapes appeared and disappeared into the mist. Although everyone had turned on their porch lights, the fog turned them into dim, glowing eyes on this dark night. What a perfect Halloween, I thought.

What is the mood that the writer creates in this passage?

A sad

B funny

(C) a little scary

D very happy

17. In the passage, the writer compares the porch lights to —

(A) glowing eyes

B tree branches

C the fog

D shapes

Achieve It! Practice Cards

_____

Research and Study Skills

A World of Information

The research to develop the Internet first began in the 1960s. Today, more than 350 million people worldwide have access to the Internet. No wonder our time in history is called the "Information Age."

In this unit you will learn ways to find and arrange information.

Shape the Topic

■ Study It

To write a report, you can **brainstorm** to pick a topic. When you brainstorm, make a list of every possible topic that comes to mind. It is not important that the topics on the list go together. Then pick one of the topics.

Sometimes a topic is too broad, or large, and covers too much information. Making a **topic web** can help you narrow your topic.

To make a topic web, ask questions about the topic. If you chose the topic of storms, for example, you could ask *What kinds of storms are there?* Then ask questions about each kind of storm, such as *What do I need to know about hurricanes?* Use a different shape for each level of your topics to keep ideas about each topic together. In the web below, notice that the main topic is in a circle; the subtopics are in rectangles; and the details are in diamonds.

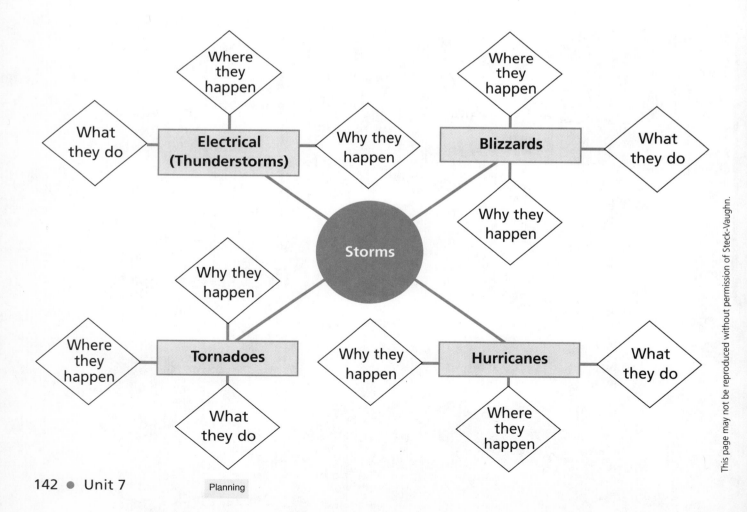

Planning

Finding subtopics helps you think about what to put in your report. The subtopic you choose will depend on

- your interests
- how easy or hard it is to find information about your subtopic
- the length of the report

A longer report might be about different kinds of storms. A shorter report might only be about one subtopic, such as hurricanes.

After you have narrowed your topic, keep asking questions to find information about the topic.

Look at the questions in the chart for a report on hurricanes.

Question Word	Report Question
Who	Who keeps track of hurricanes?
What	What happens during a hurricane?
When	When is hurricane season?
Where	Where do hurricanes form?
Why	Why do hurricanes have names?
How	How do people stay safe during hurricanes?

Make a list of questions about your topic using the six question words. Look for the answers to the questions as you read. Some questions will lead to more questions. Keep a list of the questions and the answers that you find.

Finally, decide which of the answers you want to put in your report. Remember that some information may be more important and interesting than other information you find.

Use It

Look at this topic web. It shows you how to narrow the topic of exploring space. Then answer the questions.

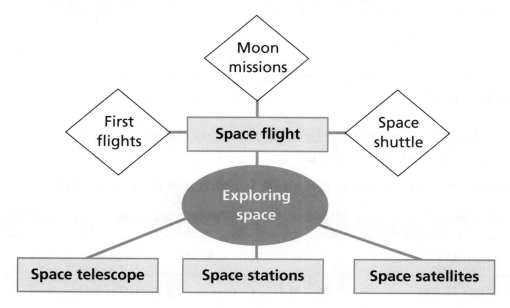

1. Which topic is broader, or larger — Exploring space or Space flight?

   _____

   _____

2. Which topic is broader, or larger — Space flight or Space shuttle?

   _____

   _____

Now read each topic on the chart. Write one more question for each topic. Start the question with a question word—who, what, when, where, why, or how.

Topics		
Chocolate	**Diamonds**	**Jazz Music**
How is chocolate made? Where does chocolate come from?	What are diamonds?	When did jazz start?

Practice It

Read each item. Circle the letter of the correct answer.

1. You want to write a report on poetry. You could narrow your topic by writing about —

    A newspapers

    B rhyme

    C pictures

    D historical fiction

2. Which question will help you write a report about important machines invented in the twentieth century?

    A When did people start riding horses?

    B What machines do we use every day?

    C How did people learn about fire?

    D Who discovered the wheel?

3. You are planning to write a report about clocks. You could narrow your topic by writing about —

    A furniture

    B wall calendars

    C pocket watches

    D train schedules

Tip Write questions to help you narrow your topic for your report.

Finding the Facts

◢ Study It

After you've chosen your topic and written your questions, you need to find the information to answer your questions. Finding information is often called doing **research.** You get your information from **sources.**

Libraries have many kinds of sources. Almanacs, atlases, books, dictionaries, encyclopedias, magazines, and newspapers are sources. Some libraries have computers. Other sources are experts on your topic who can help answer your questions. Make sure you can depend on your sources.

An **encyclopedia** is a good place to start. Most encyclopedias are in a set made up of several **volumes,** or books, in alphabetical order. Each volume has information about people, places, things, and events. **Entries,** or topics, are also in alphabetical order within each volume.

To use an encyclopedia, look for your topic alphabetically by volume. For example, you would look in Volume H for information on hurricanes. You can also look in the encyclopedia's index. The index is either at the end of the entire set of encyclopedias or in a volume by itself.

Look at this entry from an encyclopedia.

> **Guide words** are at the top of each page. They name the topic of the first article on a left-hand page and the topic of the last article on a right-hand page. Your topic will be in alphabetical order between the two guide words.

> **Entry word**
> This is the topic you are looking up.

261   Humor

Hurricane Hurricanes are powerful storms. Hurricanes form over oceans when the water temperature is warm. The heat from the water causes the storm to form. A hurricane has strong winds that travel at speeds as high as 150 miles per hour. In the Atlantic Ocean, hurricane season lasts from June through November.

Locate sources

When you write a report, you need to use more than one source. To find a book in the library, you need to understand how the books are arranged. The books in the library are classified, or put in an order called the **Dewey Decimal System.** Each book has a number that tells you what kind of information is in it and where it is in the library.

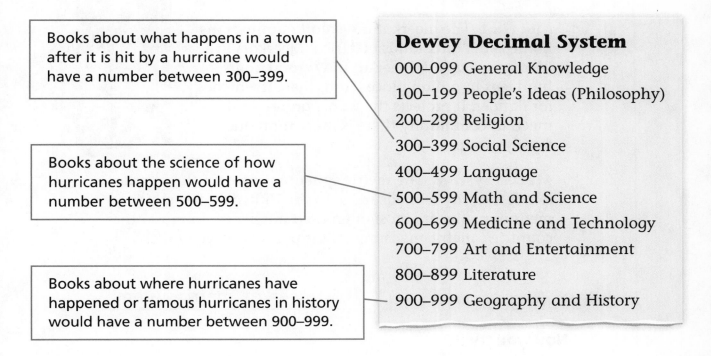

Books about what happens in a town after it is hit by a hurricane would have a number between 300–399.

Books about the science of how hurricanes happen would have a number between 500–599.

Books about where hurricanes have happened or famous hurricanes in history would have a number between 900–999.

Dewey Decimal System
000–099 General Knowledge
100–199 People's Ideas (Philosophy)
200–299 Religion
300–399 Social Science
400–499 Language
500–599 Math and Science
600–699 Medicine and Technology
700–799 Art and Entertainment
800–899 Literature
900–999 Geography and History

Find a book's number by looking in the library's card catalog under the topic or the author's last name. The catalog is in alphabetical order. The catalog may be on cards in a set of drawers in the library or stored on a computer. The information about the books is arranged in the same way on cards as it is on the computer.

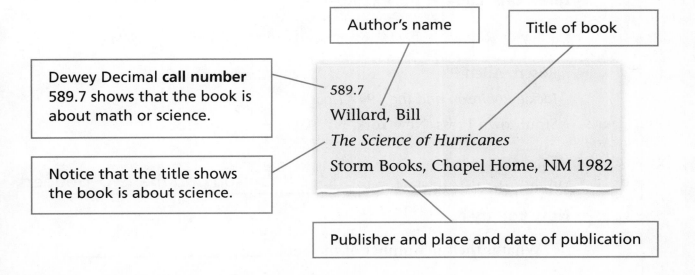

Author's name

Title of book

Dewey Decimal **call number** 589.7 shows that the book is about math or science.

Notice that the title shows the book is about science.

589.7
Willard, Bill
The Science of Hurricanes
Storm Books, Chapel Home, NM 1982

Publisher and place and date of publication

■ Use It

Look at this entry from an encyclopedia. Then answer the questions. Look at the example.

---

192   Medicine

Meerkat The meerkat is a small mammal. Its home is the grasslands of Africa. Meerkats live in large groups. A meerkat may stand on its hind legs in a high place. From there it watches for danger. It protects the whole group. In the meerkat community there is more than one family group.

Metric system The metric system is based on the number ten. It is a way of measuring. In the United States, metric measurements are most often used in science. In most other countries, metric measurement is part of everyday life.

What are the entry words? _meerkat, metric system_

Now you try it.

1. In which volume of an encyclopedia would you find information about the metric system? _____

2. What is the guide word on this page? _____

Look at this card from a card catalog. Then answer the questions. Look at the example.

942.3

Rosen, Allen P.

Jackie Robinson and the 1947 Dodgers

Smalltown Press, New York, NY 1999

What is the title of the book? _Jackie Robinson and the 1947 Dodgers_

Now you try it.

1. What is the call number of the book? _____

2. This call number is about what topic? _____

Practice It

Look at this example page from an encyclopedia. Then read the items. Circle the letter of the correct answer.

> **321   Goldfish**
>
> **Golf** Golf is a sport. The object of the game is to hit a small, hard ball along a course. The ball has to be hit into certain holes on the course. Players hit the ball with special sticks, or clubs. The winner gets the ball into all the holes with the fewest hits.
>
> **Goodall, Jane** Jane Goodall's studies about chimpanzees are world-famous. She has worked with chimpanzees for more than 40 years. She does her work in Tanzania, Africa. Goodall's findings about chimpanzees have improved the way people understand these very smart animals.

1. **What is the guide word on this page?**

   A 321

   B Goodall, Jane

   C Goldfish

   D Volume G

2. **What are entry words on this sample page?**

   A Golf and Goodall, Jane

   B chimpanzees and clubs

   C course and Tanzania, Africa

   D 321 and Golf

3. **When you look at a card from a library card catalog, the call number tells you —**

   A how many pages are in the book

   B the address where the book was published

   C the topic of the book and where to find it

   D where to buy the book

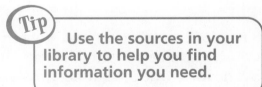

Tip Use the sources in your library to help you find information you need.

Make a Note

Study It

Before you write a report, collect information to answer your questions about the topic. Writing down this information is called **taking notes.**

When you are taking notes, write a **bibliography,** or list of the sources you use to find information. Make a note card for each source you use. Write the title, author, publisher, and year the book was published on each card. Number each source. For example, here is a note card for a source on hurricanes.

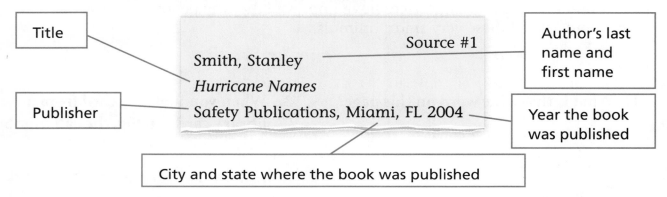

When you take notes, write a note card for each of your questions. You can **summarize,** or briefly say in your own words, the information from the source. Include on the note card the page numbers where you found the information.

Look at this passage from Source #1 above. Then look at the note card.

Since 1978 both men's and women's names have been used to name hurricanes. One reason hurricanes are named is so people can share information about them. During the Atlantic hurricane season, there can be more than one hurricane at the same time. It is important that everyone knows which storm is being talked about.

Source #1, pages 232–233
Why are hurricanes named?
More than one storm can happen at the same time. Names help people know which storm is being talked about.

Notes/summarize

Use It

Read this passage. Then look at the sample note cards. Fill in the missing information.

> **Source #2:** Earth is surrounded by layers or zones of gases. These layers make up the atmosphere. The layer closest to Earth is called the troposphere. This layer is where hurricanes form.

Source #2, page 535
What is the atmosphere?
_____

Source #2, page 535
Where do hurricanes form?
_____

Practice It

Read each item. Circle the letter of the correct answer.

1. **What would you write on your note cards for a report?**

   A the page numbers where the information was found

   B why you are interested in the topic

   C how many hours you read

   D the title of your favorite novel

2. **When you summarize information, you —**

   A copy a paragraph from a book you used

   B write questions you need to answer

   C retell the facts you have read in your own words

   D write a list of all the sources

Tip
Use note cards to summarize information that answers your questions.

Lining Up the Outline

◤ Study It

Sometimes you will be asked to write an **outline** after you have collected the information for your report. An outline helps you put the information in an order that makes sense.

Think about the questions that you asked about your topic. Put the questions in the order that will make sense to the reader. Your questions can become the main topics and subtopics in an outline.

Look at the outline below.

Title: Hurricanes

I. Introduction

> The introduction tells the reader what the report is about. It tells the main idea of the report.

II. What is a hurricane?

> Decide on the main topics of the report. Identify each main topic with a Roman numeral.

   A. Where do hurricanes form?

   B. When is "hurricane season"?

III. What happens during a hurricane?

> You might need to break a subtopic into details. Identify each detail with a number.

   A. Over the ocean

   B. Over land

> Subtopics support the main topics. Identify each subtopic with a capital letter.

     1. Causes damage

     2. Loses power

IV. Conclusion

> The conclusion retells the main idea of the report.

You may need to make changes to your outline. After you finish writing it, you may realize that another order for the information makes more sense, or that you need to add some main topics or details. Then you will need to change the order in the outline. Putting the ideas in another order can help you decide the best way to write your report.

Outline

Use It

Look at the outline. Use the items in the box to fill in the blanks in the outline.

Title: Nature in Antarctica

   I. Introduction

   II. The continent of Antarctica

       A. Southern tip of the world

          1. No daylight for six months

          2. _____

       B. Ice caps all year

   III. _____

       A. Sea birds

       B. _____

       C. _____

   IV. _____

> Bottlenose dolphins
> Antarctica's wildlife
> No darkness for six months
> River otters
> Conclusion

Practice It

Read each item. Circle the letter of the correct answer.

1. **Which two parts of an outline go together?**

   A Roman numeral and main topic

   B Roman numeral and detail

   C capital letter and main topic

   D number and subtopic

2. **The purpose of an outline is to —**

   A make the report more interesting

   B put ideas in order

   C brainstorm to find a topic

   D take notes and collect information

 Tip Use an outline to put your ideas in an order that makes sense to the reader.

Last but Not Least

◼ Study It

The last part of a report is the bibliography. A **bibliography** lists your sources. Entries are in alphabetical order with authors' last names first. The bibliography helps readers find more information.

Look at the sources listed in the bibliography entries below. Notice how punctuation marks are used.

Book

Blount, Stanley R. Atlantic Hurricanes. New York: W. W. Norton & Co., 1982.

Author   **Title**   **Place of Publication**   **Publisher**   **Date of Publication**

Underline the titles of books, newspapers, magazines, movies, or plays. On a computer, use *italics,* or slanted letters, for these titles.

Encyclopedia Article

"Hurricanes." *The Columbia Encyclopedia.* 5th ed. New York: Columbia University Press, 1993.

Article Title   **Encyclopedia Title**   **Place of Publication**   **Publisher**   **Date of Publication**

Put the title of the article first in quotation marks if the author is unknown. Underline or use *italics* for the encyclopedia title.

Magazine Article

Sado, Jack. "Safety in a Hurricane." *Storm Watcher Magazine.* 26 May 2003.

Author   **Article Title**   **Magazine Title**   **Date of Publication**

Write the author's name first. Put the article title in quotation marks. Underline or use *italics* for the magazine title.

Website

"Why Are Hurricanes Named?" *U.S. Ocean and Atmospheric Bureau.* 12 March 2003.
<http://www.usoab.gov>

Web Address   **Title of Web Article**   **Name of Website**   **Date of Publication**

References and citations

Use It

Look at these examples from a bibliography. Find what is wrong with each entry. Write your answer on the line. Look at this example.

Archer, Diane P. Run Like the Wind. Lincoln, NE: Weather Wise, 1997.

The title of the book is not underlined.

Now you try it.

1. Peterson, Marie. How to Make Your Home Safe in a Hurricane. USA Nation, August 22, 1999.

   _____

2. "Weather." Natural Encyclopedia. 7th Edition. New York: Nature's Press, 2001.

   _____

Practice It

Read each question. Circle the letter of the correct answer.

1. **How do you arrange a bibliography?**

   A by date a book or article was published

   B by number of pages

   C by alphabetical order

   D by author's first name

    Tip Write the bibliography cards for your sources when you take notes for your report.

2. **Which of the following is a correct entry for a bibliography?**

   A "Cherry Trees." The Baldwin Encyclopedia. 9th Edition. New York: Timbucktu University Press, 1996.

   B Beautiful Beaches. Gardnist, Calvin R. New York: P.G. Lartop & Co., 1978.

   C New York Mirror. Feb. 3, 1981. Flanner, Kim. "Bicycle Helmets."

   D Jill Mandel. New York: Paperback Press, 1990. Great Winds.

Unit 7
Test-Taking Strategy

Strategy: Use Your ABCs

In this unit you learned to locate sources. You learned how to use guide words at the top of a page of an encyclopedia. The guide word on the left-hand page tells the first entry on the two pages. The guide word on the right-hand page tells the last entry on the two pages.

To answer questions about whether your topic is between the guide words

- look at the beginning letter or letters of the guide words
- look at the topic you are searching for
- use alphabetical order to determine whether the topic comes between the two guide words

---

Try It Out

Read the question. Circle the letter of the correct answer.

Which topic comes between the guide words <u>teeth</u> and <u>telescope</u>?

A temperature

B television

C telephone

D tea

Look at each of the answer choices. <u>Temperature</u> begins with *tem*. *Tem* comes after *tel* in telescope. <u>Temperature</u> does not come between the two guide words. <u>Television</u> comes after the word <u>telescope</u>. It does not come between the two guide words. <u>Tea</u> comes before the word <u>teeth</u>. It does not come between the two guide words. <u>Telephone</u> comes after the word <u>teeth</u> and before the word <u>telescope</u>. So, **C** is the correct answer.

Unit 7 • Research and Study Skills
Put It to the Test

This test will check what you have learned in this unit.

DIRECTIONS: Circle the letter of the correct answer.

1. **You could narrow the topic <u>sports</u> to —**

   A board games

   B swimming

   C pizza

   D playing

2. **The purpose of a bibliography is to —**

   A tell people what your report is about

   B show what sources you used for your information

   C show people how you put your information in order

   D have more pages in your report

3. **The purpose of an outline is to —**

   A think about questions for your topic

   B use the question words

   C put your sources in order

   D put your ideas in an order that makes sense

4. **On an encyclopedia page, the guide word is the —**

   A name of the encyclopedia

   B word that names the topic

   C word at the top of the page

   D page number

5. **Where would you look in the library to find a book about healthful foods?**

   A the card catalog

   B an encyclopedia

   C a newspaper

   D a note card

6. **When you take notes from a source, it is a good idea to —**

   A make up the facts you need

   B use only one source

   C write down the information that answers your questions

   D have no clear topic in mind

GO ON

Achieve It! Practice Cards

_____

7. **What important question could you ask before you write a report about the human eye?**

   A How does the eye work?

   B Why do people have eyes?

   C How many eyes do people have?

   D Where are people's eyes?

---

p   148634.6

Pawdeer, Devorah

Helpful Home Pets: from friend to helper

Crows Branch, N.S.W.: Smith & Jones, 2012.

---

8. **The call number 634.6 tells you —**

   A how many pages are in the book

   B where to buy the book

   C the topic of the book and where to find it in a library

   D the publisher's address

9. **The first item you write for your source in a bibliography is the —**

   A date it was published

   B author's last name

   C publisher

   D illustrator's name

10. **When you take notes, you should —**

    A copy exactly what you read

    B write down all the information

    C summarize what you read in your own words

    D write down anything that is interesting

11. **Which topic belongs in a topic web about health?**

    A exercise

    B driving

    C movies

    D books

12. **Which part of an outline starts with a Roman numeral?**

    A a subtopic

    B a fact

    C a detail

    D a main topic

STOP

Achieve It! Practice Cards

_____

Writing Skills

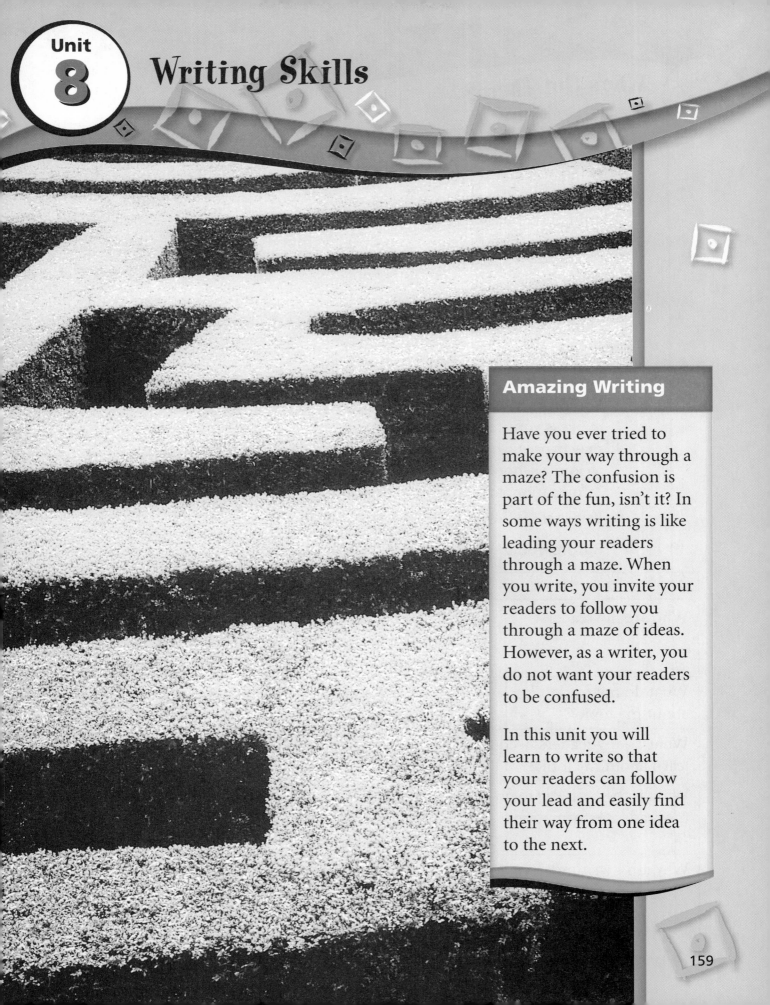

Amazing Writing

Have you ever tried to make your way through a maze? The confusion is part of the fun, isn't it? In some ways writing is like leading your readers through a maze. When you write, you invite your readers to follow you through a maze of ideas. However, as a writer, you do not want your readers to be confused.

In this unit you will learn to write so that your readers can follow your lead and easily find their way from one idea to the next.

Lesson 41

Who's Out There?

■ Study It

Whenever you write, there is always someone who will read your writing. Your friend may read a letter about your visit with your aunt and uncle. Other students may read your story in the school newspaper about cleaning up the playground. If you keep a diary or a journal, you are writing for yourself.

Your readers are your **audience.** Good writers think about their audience and make writing choices based on what they know about their audience.

Good writers also think about their **purpose,** or reason, for writing. You may write a story to **entertain** your little sister. You may write to **express** your feelings, such as in a journal or a personal letter. You may express your opinion in an essay to **persuade** other students to join a school club. You may create a flyer to **inform,** or give information, to community members about an event. Each writing task is special. Each audience is special, too.

Before you write, think about these questions.

Question	Why the Question Is Important
Who are my readers?	Different readers have different needs. You write one way for your little brother and another way for your teacher.
What do my readers know about my topic?	You want to build on what your readers already know.
What do my readers need to learn about my topic?	You want to give your readers the information they need.
What is the best way to give my readers information?	Some information can be written. Other information is easier to understand if it appears in charts or pictures.
Why am I writing?	Sometimes you write to entertain. At other times you write to express, to persuade, or to give information.

Audience/purpose

Use It

Read these items. Write what or who would probably be the BEST purpose or audience for each writing task.

teacher or another student 1. a report about rain forests (audience)

to express feelings 2. I love my grandmother's garden. It smells like summer. The tomato vines are drooping from the weight of the plump red and yellow tomatoes. (purpose)

Now you try it.

To express feeling 1. The fourth graders will present their class play next Thursday at 7:00 P.M. in the cafeteria. (purpose)

teacher or another student 2. a letter about what you did during the summer (audience)

to pesuade 3. Long ago a little elf lived under a rose bush. (purpose)

entertain 4. Vote for Amy for class president because she has a lot of experience. (purpose)

Practice It

Read this question. Circle the letter of the correct answer.

People in our community should help with the park cleanup!

What is the purpose for writing this sentence?

A (to express)

B   to give information

C   to entertain

D   to persuade

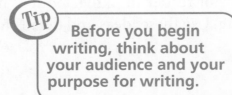

Tip
Before you begin writing, think about your audience and your purpose for writing.

42

Begin, Explain, End

◼ Study It

You want your audience to understand what you are writing. A very important part of writing is how you organize, or arrange, your ideas. The **introduction,** or beginning, will introduce the topic. The **body,** or middle, will state and explain your main ideas. The **conclusion,** or end, will complete your writing and remind your reader of the main ideas.

Much of the writing you are doing now has an introduction in the first paragraph and a conclusion in the last paragraph. The body of the writing usually has one or more paragraphs.

Look at this chart. It will help you understand how to organize your writing.

How to Organize Your Writing		
Introduction (Beginning)	**Body (Middle)**	**Conclusion (End)**
• Gets the reader's attention and makes him or her want to read the writing • Introduces the subject or topic of the writing • Shows the writer's purpose	• Explains each main idea in its own paragraph • States each main idea in a topic sentence • Supports each main idea with facts and details	• Finishes the writing • States the most important ideas and details again in different words • Leaves the reader with an interesting thought

There are generally three ways to introduce your topic. You can start with someone doing something, saying something, or thinking something, often by asking a question. Then write at least one paragraph for each main idea in the body. Be sure to support each main idea with facts and details. Decide what ideas and details you want your reader thinking about as he or she finishes reading your writing. Use these ideas and details to write your conclusion.

Introduction/body/conclusion

Read this passage. Circle the paragraph with the introduction. Put a box around the body paragraphs. Underline the paragraph with the conclusion.

Hopscotch

1 Have you ever played hopscotch? It has been around for hundreds of years. It is older than basketball. The game may have first been played in Rome.

2 Hopscotch is played on a hard surface. The board is made of numbered squares. Players hop across the squares to move back and forth on the board. Sometimes players use a stone to mark where they cannot hop. A turn ends when a player steps on a line. A turn can also end if a player falls or if his or her raised foot touches the ground.

3 The name hopscotch comes from two old words. You know that hop means "jump." The meaning of scotch comes from scratch, a word that once meant "line." In other words, players hop over a line. That is a good description, isn't it?

4 So the next time you play hopscotch, remember two things. You are playing a very old game. And remember to hop the scotch to keep your turn!

Look at this chart to see how the beginning, middle, and end of the passage work together.

Hopscotch		
Introduction	**Body**	**Conclusion**
Paragraph 1 asks a question to make readers want to continue reading.	Paragraph 2 explains the game. Paragraph 3 tells how the game got its name.	Paragraph 4 retells the two main points in different words.

Readers of this passage will be able to understand the writing because of the way it is organized. Paragraph 1 gets the reader's attention. Paragraphs 2 and 3 state and support the main ideas. Paragraph 4 restates the most important ideas and leaves the reader with an interesting thought.

Read this passage. Circle the paragraph with the introduction. Put a box around the body paragraphs. Underline the paragraph with the conclusion.

1 Not many people know John Muir's name. But we should be thankful to him. He worked hard to preserve a great treasure of the United States, the wilderness.

2 Muir, an immigrant, was born in Scotland in 1838. He moved to the United States in 1849. He lived on a farm in Wisconsin. He loved the outdoors.

3 Muir thought people should take better care of the wilderness. Famous people like President Theodore Roosevelt were interested in his ideas.

4 Because of Muir's work, the areas around Sequoia and Yosemite were set aside as national parks in 1890. Soon afterward, a national parks program began.

5 We may not have heard of John Muir, but every person who enjoys our national parks benefits from his work.

Look at this chart. Fill in what each paragraph does.

John Muir		
Introduction	**Body**	**Conclusion**

Practice It

Read this passage. Then read the questions. Circle the letter of the correct answer.

1 What did people do before there was money? They had to trade goods. This trading was called bartering.

2 This is how bartering worked. Suppose I had some meat that you wanted. You would offer to give me a shirt for the meat. If I agreed, we would trade, or barter.

3 But what if I did not want your shirt? I could be left with lots of meat that I might not need. Perhaps other people would join our barter circle. This could become hard to keep track of, couldn't it?

4 Money was invented to solve the problems with bartering. Money helps people get what they need without having to trade things. It is a good idea, isn't it?

1. **Which paragraph in the body of the passage explains the problem with bartering?**

   A paragraph 1

   B paragraph 2

   C paragraph 3

   D paragraph 4

2. **Which paragraph is the conclusion?**

   A paragraph 1

   B paragraph 2

   C paragraph 3

   D paragraph 4

Tip Organize your ideas in your writing so that you have an introduction, a body, and a conclusion.

Lesson 43

Support It!

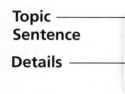 **Study It**

Every paragraph should be based on one main idea. This main idea is stated in a **topic sentence,** which is usually the first or last sentence of the paragraph. The other sentences in the paragraph give facts and details about the main idea. They **support** the main idea or topic sentence.

Read this paragraph.

Topic Sentence →
Details →

> The dictionary is a very useful book. We use it to find out how to spell words. We also use dictionaries to find out how to say words. If we want to know where a word comes from, or its origin, we can find that in a dictionary, too.

Main Idea
The dictionary is a very useful book.

Detail	Detail	Detail
We use it for spelling.	**We use it to say words correctly.**	**We can find word origins in dictionaries.**

The writer uses the topic sentence, "The dictionary is a very useful book," to introduce the main idea of the paragraph. The other sentences provide facts about a dictionary. These sentences explain why a dictionary is a useful book. They support the main idea.

Sometimes a writer will choose to put the topic sentence at the end of the paragraph. Then the topic sentence ties the details together. As a writer you will make the choice that is best for each paragraph.

All of the sentences in a paragraph should be related to each other. They work together to give your reader information.

Main idea/supporting details

Read this passage.

The setting of this book is an old farm. The author's descriptions made me feel as though I were there. The characters seem very real, especially the ten-year-old twins. Like me, they get into trouble. The action in the book is also very real. The twins have a map and go looking for their grandfather's treasure. All in all, this is an excellent adventure book.

Look at this chart. Notice how the details are used to support the main idea.

Main Idea
This is an excellent adventure book.

Detail	Detail	Detail
The descriptions make the reader feel as though he or she is there.	The twins get into trouble, just as real people do.	The twins use a map to find their grandfather's treasure.

Where is the topic sentence in this paragraph? This writer put it at the end of the paragraph. The writer chose to discuss the details of the book before giving an opinion about the book as a whole.

◤ Use It

Read this paragraph.

You may not think about it, but packages play a big part in your life. Think about a trip to the grocery store. Colorful cardboard packages help you find your favorite cereal. Honey, a liquid, is easier to handle because it is in a jar. Milk is kept clean and fresh because of its container. Soap and other cleaning products are wrapped in packages that keep their scents away from food items.

Fill in the chart with details that support the main idea.

Main Idea
Packages play a big part in your life.

Detail	Detail	Detail	Detail

Read each question. Write your answer on the line.

1. Where is the topic sentence in this paragraph?

   _____

2. Why do you think the writer chose to put the topic sentence in this place?

   _____

   _____

   _____

   _____

Practice It

Read this paragraph. Then read each item. Circle the letter of the correct answer.

Cotton is one of the world's most useful plants. In many countries people have jobs growing cotton or working with it. A lot of clothing is made from cotton. Other cotton products we use include rugs, curtains, and towels. Cotton even provides cottonseed oil, which is used in cooking!

1. **What is the topic sentence of this paragraph?**

   A Cotton is one of the world's most useful plants.

   B In many countries people have jobs growing cotton or working with it.

   C Clothing is made from cotton.

   D Cotton even provides cottonseed oil, which is used in cooking!

2. **Look at this chart.**

Main Idea
Cotton is one of the world's most useful plants.

Detail	Detail	Detail	Detail
Cotton provides jobs.	**Clothes are made from cotton.**		**Cooking oil is made from cotton.**

   Which detail from the paragraph should be added to the chart?

   A Cotton is grown on plants.

   B Socks and shirts are made from cotton.

   C Rugs, curtains, and towels are made from cotton.

   D Cotton is a good fabric for summer.

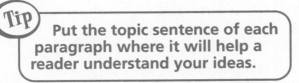

Tip Put the topic sentence of each paragraph where it will help a reader understand your ideas.

Tell It Well

◢ Study It

Good writers connect ideas well. Readers should be able to follow one idea to the next easily, without a lot of questions or confusion.

Look at this chart. It shows three ways to improve your writing.

Add	Look for places to add main ideas, facts, or details that will make your writing clearer to the reader. You can also add sequence, or time order, words to help the reader move from one idea to the next. Some sequence words include <u>once</u>, <u>before</u>, <u>first</u>, <u>next</u>, <u>then</u>, <u>after</u>, <u>last</u>, and <u>finally</u>.
Remove	Take out words, sentences, or paragraphs that are not related to the topic or that simply repeat information.
Combine	Rewrite short, choppy sentences into one longer sentence. Also combine repeated information into one clear sentence or paragraph.

Read this paragraph.

    <u>First</u>, Ramon got his backpack out of the closet. He threw three pairs of socks into it. <u>Then</u>, he put in pajamas and some t-shirts. <u>Next</u>, he folded jeans and added them to the pack. <u>Finally</u>, he threw in his favorite book and a toothbrush. He ran downstairs and called, "I'm ready to go camping!"

This paragraph is about how Ramon gets ready for his camping trip. The writer added sequence words to help you move from one event to the next.

Coherence

Read this paragraph.

   (1) Tyrone liked riding the bus to school. (2) He was at the bus stop on time every morning. (3) Buses are a very popular way for students to get to school. (4) He waited with his friends Jimmy and Kezia. (5) They would tell jokes and talk about their homework. (6) On the bus Tyrone usually sat with Ben. (7) They studied together for tests. (8) All in all, it was a good way to start the day.

This paragraph is about Tyrone and his experiences on the school bus. Most of the sentences support this topic. However, sentence 3 is about buses in general and not about Tyrone's school bus. It is not related to the topic and needs to be removed from the paragraph.

Read this paragraph.

   (1) Moths and butterflies are very much alike. (2) Moths are insects. (3) Butterflies are insects.(4) Moths have four wings. (5) Butterflies have four wings. (6) Moths collect nectar from flowers. (7) Butterflies collect nectar from flowers. (8) Moths take pollen from flower to flower. (9) Butterflies take pollen from flower to flower.

This paragraph is about the similarities between moths and butterflies. This passage is hard to read because many words are repeated. Also, the sentences are short and choppy. The writing improves when you combine some of the sentences and remove the words that are repeated. For example, sentences 2 through 5 could be combined into the sentence <u>Both moths and butterflies are insects with four wings.</u>

◢ Use It

Read this passage.

Two favorite dishes, spaghetti with tomato sauce and macaroni and cheese, are very similar foods. The sauce for spaghetti is usually made with tomatoes. This makes a spicy dish. Both meals are very good.

1. What information should be added to this passage?

   _____

Read this passage.

(1) Benjamin Franklin left a special mark on the city of Philadelphia. (2) He started the first public library in America. (3) He began a firefighting company. (4) He also lived in France for a while.

2. Which sentence should be removed from this passage?

   _____

3. Why should this sentence be removed?

   _____

   _____

Read this passage.

Macaroni is a noodle. To make macaroni and cheese, first add cheese to the cooked noodles. Then add butter and milk.

4. Identify the sequence words used in this passage.

   _____

5. Combine the sentences in this passage to make one sentence.

   _____

   _____

Practice It

Read this paragraph. Then read each item. Circle the letter of the correct answer.

(1) The milk that you buy from a store has taken quite a journey. (2) Then it is cooled and taken to a dairy to be prepared. (3) At the dairy the milk is heated to kill any bacteria in it. (4) Next, the cream is removed from the milk. (5) The cream is packaged separately. (6) This keeps any fat in the milk from rising to the top. (7) The milk is then sent through a machine with many tiny holes. (8) Finally, the milk is packaged and sent to the store. (9) You should drink three glasses of milk each day.

1. **Which sentence does NOT belong in this paragraph?**

   A sentence 9

   B sentence 2

   C sentence 7

   D sentence 8

2. **Which of these is the BEST way to combine sentences 4 and 5?**

   A The cream is packaged after the milk is removed.

   B First, remove the milk. Then, package the cream.

   C Next, the cream is removed from the milk and packaged separately.

   D The cream and the milk are packaged together.

3. **Which sentence could BEST be added after sentence 1?**

   A The milk is collected on a farm.

   B Most people buy milk at a grocery store.

   C Trucks are used to take milk from one state to another.

   D Milk is a good source of calcium.

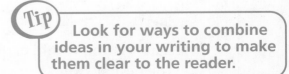

Tip

Look for ways to combine ideas in your writing to make them clear to the reader.

Unit 8
Test-Taking Strategy

Strategy: Determine Purpose and Audience

In this unit you learned to identify different purposes for writing and different kinds of audiences. When you are asked about writing tasks on a test, ask yourself

- What is the purpose of this piece of writing? Is it to entertain, to express, to persuade, or to inform?

- Who will read this piece of writing? Is it for friends, for a teacher, or for someone else?

Try It Out

Read these questions. Circle the letter of the correct answer.

> Explain how to make something. Include enough information so that your reader will understand how to make the thing.

1. **What is the purpose of this writing task?**

   A to entertain

   B to persuade

   C to inform

   D to express

The purpose is to inform someone about making something, so **C** is the best answer.

2. **Who would probably be the audience for this piece of writing?**

   A a newspaper editor

   B a teacher

   C a baby brother

   D a student

The writing would explain to a student how to do something, so **D** is the best answer.

Name _____

Unit 8 • Writing Skills
Put It to the Test

This test will check what you have learned in this unit.

**DIRECTIONS: Read this passage. Then read each item.
Circle the letter of the correct answer.**

Two Heroes

(1) Pecos Bill was a legendary cowboy. (2) As a baby he was raised by coyotes. (3) When he grew up, his strength was well known. (4) Instead of a horse, he rode a mountain lion. (5) He also used a rattlesnake for a whip. (6) Once, during a dry spell, Pecos Bill drained a river to water his ranch. (7) It has been said that cowboys told stories about him each evening as they gathered at the campfire. (8) These stories always talked about Bill's quick thinking and courage. (9) Bill's wife, Slue-foot Sue, was also part of the stories.

(10) Paul Bunyan was a legend, too. (11) However, he was famous in the American forests. (12) He was a lumberjack. (13) Paul could cut down two trees at once. (14) The Great Lakes were formed from his footprints. (15) His companion was Babe, a big blue ox. (16) Babe could pull entire forests to the lumber mill in one trip. (17) Lumberjacks traded Paul Bunyan stories in their camps at night. (18) Stories about Paul Bunyan told of his power and speed.

1. **What is the passage MAINLY about?**

   A Coyotes are smart and make good parents.

   B Cowboys are clever and courageous.

   C Heroes in legends have qualities that people admire.

   D Large oxen once lived in America.

2. **In the second paragraph, sentence 10 is —**

   A an important detail in the paragraph

   B the main idea of the paragraph

   C a definition in the paragraph

   D the purpose of the paragraph

Achieve It! Practice Cards

_____

This page may not be reproduced without permission of Steck-Vaughn.

3. The writer uses the words <u>once</u>, <u>too</u>, and <u>when</u> in the passage. What are these words called?

    A sequence words

    B cause and effect words

    C comparison and contrast words

    D descriptive words

4. What is the purpose of "Two Heroes"?

    A to describe ranches

    B to give information about folk legends

    C to entertain people around a campfire

    D to persuade people to become lumberjacks

5. This passage is from the middle of a report on legends. What is the middle of a report called?

    A the title

    B the introduction

    C the conclusion

    D the body

6. Who would probably be the audience for this report about two heroes?

    A the mayor and city council

    B your teacher and other students

    C your baby brother and sister

    D your aunt and uncle

7. Which sentence does NOT belong in the first paragraph?

    A sentence 2

    B sentence 5

    C sentence 7

    D sentence 9

8. Sentences that are not related to the topic should be —

    A removed from the paragraph

    B moved to another paragraph

    C combined with other sentences

    D added to another paragraph

9. What should you do with short, choppy sentences in a paragraph?

    A remove them

    B move them

    C add to them

    D combine them

Achieve It! Practice Cards

_____

Kinds of Writing

The "Write" Way

You read stories, poems, and articles in the newspaper or magazines all the time. They are written by other people. But you can write your own real or imaginary story. You can describe something that happened to you in a personal narrative. In a persuasive piece, you can try to change someone's opinion. Or maybe you need to give someone else directions for how to make or do something.

In this unit you will learn about different kinds of writing and the elements of each of them. There are so many ways to write!

What Happens Next?

◣ Study It

Are you a fan of science fiction, adventures, mysteries, or true stories? **Narratives** come in many forms. Some narratives are made up. Other narratives, such as a newspaper article or another kind of true story have facts. You can write a narrative that describes events as you remember them, such as what happened on a trip you took. You can also make up a narrative that comes from your imagination. But no matter where the narrative comes from or what type of narrative it is, a narrative needs to have an **order of events.** The narrative should have a beginning, a middle, and an end.

- What happens first?
- What happens next?
- What happens after that?
- How does the story end?

If your narrative is a fictional story, it will usually have other parts, or **elements.** A fictional story has **characters.** It also has a **plot,** or problem, and a conclusion that solves the problem. Fictional stories also have **settings,** or a time and place where the story's events happen.

Read the story. Think about elements in the story and the order of events.

On Saturday Samantha woke up with a start. Why, she wondered, was she awake so early?

Then she remembered. Today was the day of the big track meet. She had been training for this for weeks.

Jumping out of bed, she put on her running clothes and grabbed her sneakers. She ran downstairs to find her father putting breakfast on the table.

"Thanks, Dad," Samantha said. She ate breakfast and brushed her teeth before pulling on her sneakers and tying them. "I'm ready to run!"

Samantha is the main character of the story. The events that happen to her are the action in the story. Her problem is solved because she knows she is prepared for the track meet. The order of events keeps the story moving in a way that makes sense.

Narratives/stories

One kind of narrative is called a **personal narrative.** A personal narrative is a true story about something that happened to the person writing the story. The story often tells about an event and the author's ideas or thoughts about it. Usually an author describes his or her feelings in a personal narrative.

Read this personal narrative. Look for the parts of the story. Think about who is telling the story.

It was the last weekend of summer. Mario and I had been planning to camp out for weeks. Mario's backyard was the perfect place. There were so many trees that the yard seemed like a forest. A small creek even ran through it.

For days I had been feeling a little nervous about just the two of us sleeping outdoors all night. I was afraid that Mario would make fun of me if I said I was scared.

On Saturday morning Mario said, "Hey Daniel, is it OK if my dad camps out with us?"

"What a great idea!" I told him.

This story is a personal narrative because it is based on an event that happened to the author. The author, Daniel, is telling about his experience. He uses the word I to signal a personal story. Sometimes an author uses I in an imagined story, too.

Read this story. Look at the example. Then read the questions. Write the answers on the lines.

On Saturday morning Roland was in his room. He was wildly pulling things out of his closet. He had already checked under his bed. His library book was due today. He wanted to take it back so that he could get another book.

Roland was getting more and more worried that he would never find the book. He had searched everywhere. As he was looking through the books on his shelves, he heard his bedroom door open. When he turned around, he saw his dog Champ. Champ was gently carrying Roland's library book in his mouth.

"You're a great pal," Roland told Champ.

What is the first event in the story?
Roland wildly pulls things out of his closet.

Now you try it.

1. What would make the story a personal narrative?

   _____

   _____

2. What is the setting of the story?

   _____

   _____

3. In the conclusion how is the problem solved?

   _____

4. What happens right after Roland has searched everywhere?

   _____

   _____

▪ Practice It

Read the story. Then read the items. Circle the letter of the correct answer.

Olga lived in Chicago, Illinois. Her family lived close to the museum. One morning her friend Liza called to ask her to ride over to the museum. There was a new teddy bear exhibit that they both wanted to see.

After asking permission, Olga grabbed her bicycle helmet and ran outside. Then she saw it. The back tire of her bicycle was completely flat. Olga rushed into the house. Her mother was just leaving for the store.

"Could you please take me to the museum?" Olga asked.

"Hop in!" said her mother, opening the car door.

1. **What is the first event in the story?**

   A Olga lived in Chicago, Illinois.

   B Her family lived close to the museum.

   C Liza called Olga to ask her to ride over to the museum.

   D They both wanted to see the new teddy bear exhibit.

2. **How is Olga's problem solved?**

   A Liza invited her to the teddy bear exhibit.

   B Olga grabbed her bicycle helmet.

   C Olga's bicycle tire was flat.

   D Olga's mother agreed to give her a ride.

3. **Which is the BEST clue that this story takes place in present time?**

   A Chicago, Illinois

   B the museum

   C the teddy bear exhibit

   D the car door

 When you write a narrative, be sure to tell the events in an order that makes sense.

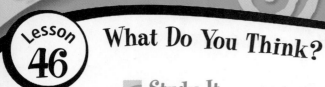

What Do You Think?

Study It

When you read, you bring your own experiences and thoughts to the story to help you understand it.

You and a friend may have completely different views of a story that both of you have read. For example, you may think that the main character is brave. Your friend may think the character is foolish for taking too many chances.

After you read a story, you may want to **respond,** or write about it, to help others understand your point of view. First, write the story's title and the author's name. If there are pictures with the story, write the name of the person who drew them, too.

When you write your thoughts about the story itself, include examples from the story to support your ideas. Like any good essay, a written response should have an introduction, a body, and a conclusion. The introduction should state the main idea of your response. The body should give details from the story about the setting, the main character, and events from the plot that support your main idea. The conclusion should restate the main idea.

Read the following passage from "The Secret Unicorn" by Lloydene Cook. Look for story elements to use for writing a response.

Tiffany reached out slowly and petted the goat's head. "What's your name?" she asked. "Where did you come from?"

"BAAA. BAAA," the goat answered, backing into the corner.

"Don't be afraid. I won't hurt you," Tiffany said.

Tiffany closed the shed door and went inside to tell her mother about the goat. "Let's go for a drive," said her mother. "Maybe we can find out who's missing a goat."

A few miles down the road they saw a farmhouse and— another goat eating grass in the pasture.

Tiffany and her mother knocked on the door of the house.

Response to literature

A chart can help you organize the important parts of the story.

Title: "The Secret Unicorn"

Author: Lloydene Cook

Parts of a Story	Examples from Story
Main Characters: Tiffany: kind and caring Mother: helpful and supportive	She is worried about the lost goat. She drives Tiffany to find the goat's owner.
Setting: Tiffany's house	Tiffany goes into her house to find her mother.
Problem: Lost goat	Tiffany asks the goat, "Where did you come from?"
Solution: Looks for the owner	The characters find a house that has another goat.

Your written response should include these important parts of the story, supported by details or examples.

Look at one reader's response to the story.

> In "The Secret Unicorn," Tiffany lives in the country with her mother. Tiffany is a kind and caring person. I know this because she finds a lost goat and wants to help it find its home. She talks very nicely to the goat. She probably likes animals because she isn't afraid to pet the goat. She asks her mother to help her find the goat's home.
>
> They find a house that has another goat in the yard. They think that the lost goat might live there. Tiffany and her mother knock on the door to ask.

Read the following passage from *The BFG* by Roald Dahl. Circle the main characters. Underline words that tell about the setting.

She saw the Giant step back a pace and put the suitcase down on the pavement. He bent over and opened the suitcase. He took something out of it. It looked like a glass jar, one of those square ones with a screw top. He unscrewed the top of the jar and poured what was in it into the end of the long trumpet thing.

Sophie watched, trembling.

She saw the Giant straighten up again and she saw him poke the trumpet in through the open upstairs window of the room where the Goochey children were sleeping. She saw the Giant take a deep breath and *whoof*, he blew through the trumpet.

Look at the chart. Fill in the missing information.

Title: _____

Author: Roald Dahl

Parts of a Story	Examples from Story
Main Characters: Giant, _____	Sophie watches the Giant.
Setting: nighttime	_____
Problem: _____ _____	Sophie sees the Giant blow stuff into the Goochey children's window.

◢ Practice It

Read the story. Then read the questions. Circle the letter of the correct answer.

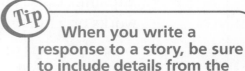

For the past two nights, Roberta had heard giggles and other sounds coming from the shed. She asked her mom about it, but her mom hadn't heard anything.

Roberta decided to wait near the shed one evening to find out what was making the sounds. When she heard the giggling, she peeked around the door. Two raccoons ran around on top of the garbage cans. They sounded as though they were giggling. Roberta crept away to get her mom.

1. **A written response should include —**

   A an introduction

   B all of the details from the story

   C a picture from the story

   D facts about the author

> **Tip**
> When you write a response to a story, be sure to include details from the story to support your ideas.

2. **Look at the chart.**

Parts of a Story	Examples from Story
Main Characters: Roberta	Roberta hears sounds.
Setting: nighttime	She hears sounds at night.
Problem: Roberta hears sounds in the shed.	
Solution: Raccoons make the noise.	Roberta sees raccoons playing on the garbage cans.

What detail is missing from the chart?

A Roberta knows that her brothers make the sounds.

B Roberta hides and watches to see what makes the sounds.

C Roberta is dreaming.

D Roberta's mother is cleaning the shed.

Tell Me About It

Study It

Suppose that you want to explain why a volcano erupts, or blows up. Maybe you want to give directions to explain how to make a model volcano.

Expository writing explains something or gives information to the reader. You can organize the information in different ways.

- Compare and contrast—You can explain how two things are alike and how they are different.
- "How to" do or make something—You can describe, step by step, how to make a snack or build a birdhouse, for example.
- Explain a cause and its effect—You can explain how something works or why something happens.
- Give directions on how to get somewhere—You can give simple directions in a list, or you can describe directions in more detail.

Before you write, plan how you want to show your information.

Look at this plan to explain how to make a peanut butter and jelly sandwich.

Plan for Writing Directions	
Topic Sentence: You can make a delicious peanut butter and jelly sandwich in minutes!	
Things Needed	**Steps to Follow**
<ul><li>two slices of bread</li><li>peanut butter</li><li>jelly</li><li>dull knife to spread peanut butter</li><li>spoon for jelly</li></ul>	**Step 1** First, put the slices of bread on a napkin or plate. **Step 2** Next, carefully spread peanut butter on one slice. **Step 3** Then, spoon some jelly onto the other slice of bread. Spread it around. **Step 4** Pick up the slice of bread with peanut butter and place it, peanut-butter-side down, on top of the other slice. **Step 5** Finally, eat the sandwich!

Expository writing

You can also use expository writing to explain a cause and effect. In this kind of writing, the author gives only the facts. The author's opinion or feelings about the topic are usually not in the passage.

The author begins with a topic. Then he or she gives details that explain how something happens. The author explains what happens and what causes that effect to happen. This kind of writing usually answers Who?, What?, When?, Where?, How?, and Why?

Read this passage. Think about how the author has organized the information.

> It starts with a tickle. Your eyes water. Your mouth opens. Ah . . . Ah . . . Ah-choo!
>
> You know how a sneeze feels, but do you know why we sneeze?
>
> Sneezing is the body's way of getting rid of something that is bothering the nose. When something starts to bother the inside of the nose, a message is sent to the brain. The brain tells the body to get rid of the bothersome thing. Then air is forced out of the nose and mouth at great speed.
>
> A sneeze is a reflex, or an action that happens automatically. You cannot control the action. Dust and pepper are some things that can cause you to sneeze. Some people sneeze when they go out into the sunlight or look at a bright light!

This passage answers the question "Why do we sneeze?"

Cause	Effect
Something starts to bother the inside of the nose.	A message is sent to the brain.
The brain tells the body to get rid of the bothersome thing.	Air is forced out of the nose and mouth at great speed.
Dust, pepper, sunlight, bright light	You may sneeze.

Use It

Read this passage. Underline the words used to compare and contrast.

Children have different ways to get around today. Two of these ways are bikes and scooters. These are alike in many ways. Both have been around for many years, but scooters have become more popular recently. You need to pedal with two feet to ride a bike. On a scooter you just push with one foot. It takes good balance to ride both bikes and scooters. However, a scooter may be a little easier to learn to ride.

Look at the chart.

Bikes
1. hard to learn
2. _____

Both
1. ride them
2. _____
3. need to balance

Scooters
1. _____
2. push with one foot
3. recently became popular

1. What information is missing under "Bikes"?

   _____

2. What information is missing under "Both"?

   _____

3. What information is missing under "Scooters"?

   _____

◤ Practice It

Read this passage from *Breathing* by John Gaskin. Then read each item. Circle the letter of the correct answer.

The air is made up of lots of different gases mixed together. There's only one that your body needs. It's called oxygen.

Each time you breathe in, your body takes the useful oxygen from the air. It sends the oxygen to all parts of your body.

As your body uses up the oxygen, it makes a waste gas. It is called carbon dioxide. Your body doesn't need this gas, so you get rid of it by breathing out.

Your body needs oxygen all the time. It takes just the right amount from the air you breathe.

1. **This passage is expository because it —**

    A describes a place

    B gives an opinion

    C gives information

    D tells a story

2. **What method did the writer use to organize the information in this passage?**

    A comparison and contrast

    B "how to" do something

    C description of the writer's opinion

    D cause and effect

> **Tip**
> If the purpose of a piece of writing is to give information, you know that the piece is an example of expository writing.

Change Your Mind

Study It

People try to get others to do things all the time. Ads in the newspaper and on TV are meant to persuade you to buy something or to go somewhere. You may try to talk a friend into letting you borrow her bike.

When you have a strong opinion or belief that you want someone else to share, you try to **persuade.** When you write to persuade, you give your opinion about something. Then you give evidence or reasons for your reader to agree with your opinion and take action. You want the reader to agree with you and act in a certain way.

When you write to persuade, you should

- clearly state your opinion in the first paragraph
- give reasons and details about why the reader should agree with your opinion
- retell your opinion and let the reader know what action you want taken and when you want it done

Read this persuasive passage.

I think it is important for our family to have a dog. We have never had a dog before. Dogs make great pets because they are friendly.

Many of my friends have dogs, and I think I am old enough to take care of one, too. I can get exercise while I walk it every day. Exercise is good for me, and the dog would help me get it. If we got a big dog, it could protect our house.

A family dog would be a great thing to have. I would like to have a family meeting right away to talk about getting one.

Persuasive writing

Notice how the writer follows the steps in writing to persuade.

1. The writer clearly states an opinion in the first paragraph.

   I think it is important for our family to have a dog.

2. The writer gives reasons for getting a dog.

   Dogs make great pets.

   He or she would get exercise when walking the dog.

   A dog could protect the family's home.

3. The writer retells the opinion and states the action that he or she wants to have happen.

   A family dog would be a great thing to have.

   I would like to have a family meeting right away.

Read this persuasive passage.

Most schools offer P. E., or physical education, as an important part of learning. P. E. classes help us stay healthy. Yet our school does not offer one of the best physical activities, swimming, because we don't have a pool. Our school needs a pool for a number of reasons.

Swimming exercises every muscle in the body. Swimming is also a skill that could save a life someday. During the summer the entire city could use the pool for exercise and for classes that teach swimming.

At the next school board meeting, I urge the members to discuss building a pool at our school.

Opinion	Reasons	Action
Our school needs a pool.	1. good exercise 2. swimming lessons 3. used by the whole town	School board should discuss building a pool.

In this passage the writer's opinion is clear. There are reasons and details to support the opinion. The last sentence tells what action the writer would like to have happen.

Use It

Read this persuasive passage. Put a box around the writer's opinion. Underline the reasons for the opinion. Circle the action that the writer hopes will happen.

Going to the public library is a lot of fun. The library has many exciting books. Everyone should get a library card.

If you have a library card, you can check out books, tapes, and movies. Some libraries have reading programs during the summer. If you read a lot of books, you might get a prize. Libraries have story time and visits from authors. You might find computers in the library, too. The library is a great place to learn how to use a computer.

Books are exciting and libraries are the place to find them. If I were you, I would get a library card right away!

Fill in the blanks with the missing reasons and action.

Opinion	Reasons	Action
Everyone should get a library card.	1. check out books, tapes, movies 2. _____ _____ 3. a prize 4. story time 5. _____ _____ 6. computers	_____ _____

Practice It

Read this persuasive passage. Then read the questions. Circle the letter of the correct answer.

All students should belong to an after-school club. No matter what you are interested in, there is something fun you can do after school.

Being part of a club is exciting. You can share the same interests with other students. If you like to play chess, you can join the chess club. Students who like to be active can join the dance group.

No matter what you like to do, there is a club for you. Sign up today and become part of an after-school club.

1. **A persuasive passage should always have —**

   A main characters

   B reasons for the opinion

   C descriptive words

   D a setting

2. **What is the writer's opinion in this passage?**

   A Students like to have fun.

   B Students have many different interests.

   C You should be part of the chess club.

   D Every student should join an after-school club.

Tip When you write to persuade, be sure to give reasons for your opinion.

Test-Taking Strategy

Strategy: Look for Story Elements

In this unit you learned that narratives have certain elements.

- characters
- setting
- problem or plot
- solution

When you read questions on a test about a story, ask yourself *Who is this story mostly about? Where does the story take place? What is the problem or the plot? How is the problem solved?*

Try It Out

Read the story. Look for the story elements. Then read the item. Circle the letter of the correct answer.

Gabriella, Erica, and Aaron had gone to the park to play baseball. Erica was at bat. She hit the ball hard. Then there was a loud crash that sounded like breaking glass.

Just then Ms. Givens drove up to the park. A window in her car was broken. "Which one of you hit that ball?" she asked.

"I did," said Erica. "I'm really sorry. I don't have money to pay for a new car window."

"That's OK," said Ms. Givens. "Maybe you can come by my house tomorrow and help paint my fence instead."

"I'll be there," said Erica.

What is the problem in this story?

A Erica has broken Ms. Givens's window.

B There is no place to play baseball.

C Ms. Givens needs help painting her fence.

D Gabriella has lost her baseball mitt.

Think about what happens in the story. The friends heard a crash after Erica hit the ball. The ball had hit Ms. Givens's car window and broken it. So, **A** is the correct answer.

Put It to the Test

Name _____

This test will check what you have learned in this unit.

DIRECTIONS: Read the passage. Circle the letter of the correct answer.

Sign Up Now

This year will be the best ever at summer camp. At Camp ChiChiWa, we will be having lots of fun. Campers will learn to canoe and fish. If you like cooking, there will be a special class for young chefs. For those campers who like to hike, our trails promise lots of exercise and wildlife. Our new cabins have bunk beds and showers. No more hiking across camp to get clean!

Our counselors have planned many craft classes from papermaking to painting. They have lots of hikes planned. Our counselors are full of energy and tell good stories. Plus, they are all trained in CPR and water safety.

So if you don't have plans for this summer, ask your parents to sign you up for a week of fun at Camp ChiChiWa. See you there!

1. **The purpose of this passage is to —**

   A give facts about craft classes

   B give directions to the camp

   C persuade you to go to camp

   D tell a story about camp

2. **What action does the writer want you to take?**

   A learn to canoe

   B take a chef's class

   C have a fun summer

   D talk to your parents

3. **This passage gives information about —**

   A a summer camp

   B water safety

   C exercise

   D hiking

GO ON

Achieve It! Practice Cards

_____

4. **Which sentence tells you the writer's opinion about the camp?**

   A Campers will learn to canoe and fish.

   B No more hiking across camp to get clean!

   C Plus, they are all trained in CPR and water safety.

   D This year will be the best ever at summer camp.

5. **What is the main idea of this passage?**

   A This summer will be the best ever at Camp ChiChiWa.

   B Camp ChiChiWa offers all kinds of classes.

   C Children should ask parents to sign them up for camp.

   D The counselors are trained in CPR and water safety.

6. **What is one of the details in this passage?**

   A Campers will learn to canoe and fish.

   B All campers need sunscreen.

   C Campers must know how to swim.

   D Campers will hike two miles every day.

7. **What sentence might be included in a written response to this passage?**

   A Most children do not like camp.

   B This camp is too far away.

   C I think this camp sounds like a lot of fun.

   D Camp is for younger children.

8. **Who would be the best audience for this passage?**

   A children who like to stay at home

   B parents who want to go to camp

   C teachers who want to be counselors

   D children who like camp

9. **The conclusion in an expository passage should —**

   A include an introduction

   B restate the main idea

   C have a lot of details

   D state an opinion

GO ON

Achieve It! Practice Cards

10. **When you respond to a story, you should include —**

   A   a lengthy conclusion

   B   the author's picture

   C   an introduction and setting

   D   details about the characters, the setting, and the plot

11. **The conclusion of a story usually —**

   A   gives the author's name

   B   tells the problem of the story

   C   tells the solution to the problem

   D   describes the main characters

12. **You would use expository writing to —**

   A   tell a story

   B   give information about a topic

   C   write a thank-you note

   D   write a poem

13. **If you wanted to explain how dogs and cats are alike and different as pets, you could organize the information using —**

   A   cause and effect

   B   comparison and contrast

   C   directions

   D   persuasion

14. **When you respond to a story, you want the reader to understand —**

   A   who your favorite author is

   B   how many books you read this year

   C   your favorite kind of poetry

   D   your point of view about the story

15. **A passage that gives directions would probably use the words —**

   A   both, unlike, like

   B   because, if, why

   C   first, next, then

   D   who, when, how

GO ON

Achieve It! Practice Cards

No Soup for Me!

One day I said to my grandmother, "Let's help out at the soup kitchen downtown." We walked to the kitchen on Saturday morning.

I thought I would just hand out bowls of soup. Everybody would thank me and think I was so helpful. Was I surprised!

Instead of serving soup, I wound up washing and peeling a mountain of potatoes. It took hours. My hands got sore and wrinkly. I kept dropping potatoes. People yelled, "Hurry up! We need potatoes for the soup!"

I never got to serve a bowl of soup. At the end of the day, my grandmother said, "Lisa, I'm hungry. What should we eat?" I cried, "Anything but soup or potatoes!"

16. This story is a —

   A reader's response

   B personal narrative

   C set of directions

   D persuasive passage

17. "Saturday morning" tells you about the story's —

   A plot

   B characters

   C setting

   D problem

18. The first thing Lisa and her grandmother do in this story is —

   A decide to help at the soup kitchen

   B wash and peel potatoes

   C hand out bowls of soup

   D eat soup and potatoes for dinner

19. Which words from the story BEST tell time order?

   A One day

   B Hurry up

   C Instead

   D At the end of the day

STOP

Achieve It! Practice Cards

_____

Language Rules

The Writing Game

The first chess game was probably played in the sixth century. By the nineteenth century, the rules of chess were still changing. When people play chess, everyone has to follow the same rules. If someone breaks the rules in chess, the game will not be enjoyable. It is the same with writing. If you do not follow the rules of language when you are writing, readers will not like or understand what you have written.

In this unit you will learn several language rules. These rules will help you write clear sentences so that people will understand your ideas and enjoy reading what you write.

Word Work

◼ Study It

Each word in a sentence is a **part of speech.** Each part of speech does a different job in a sentence. Understanding a word's job will help you use words correctly.

The main parts of speech are **nouns, pronouns, adjectives, verbs, adverbs, prepositions,** and **conjunctions.**

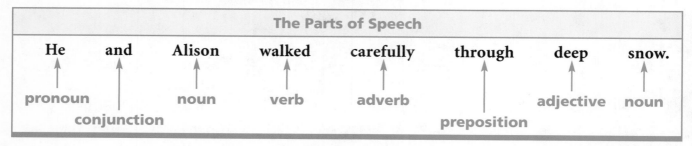

The Parts of Speech

He — pronoun
and — conjunction
Alison — noun
walked — verb
carefully — adverb
through — preposition
deep — adjective
snow. — noun

Noun: A **noun** is a person, place, or thing.

> **Alison** used her **snowboard** in **Vermont** when she visited **Matt.**

Pronoun: A **pronoun** also names people or things. A pronoun takes the place of a noun.

Three forms of pronouns are subject pronouns, object pronouns, and possessive pronouns.

- Subject pronouns take the place of the subject. I, you, he, she, it, we, they, and who are subject pronouns.

  > When Alison was in Vermont, **she** tried the new snowboard.

- Object pronouns take the place of a noun that follows an action verb. Object pronouns include me, you, him, her, it, us, them, and whom.

  > Matt tried the snowboard, too. He liked **it.**

- Possessive pronouns show ownership. My, your, his, her, its, our, and their are possessive pronouns that tell to whom or what something belongs.

  > Matt said, "I like the way **your** snowboard feels under **my** feet."

Mine, yours, his, hers, ours, and theirs are possessive pronouns that stand alone.

> "I wish I had a snowboard like **yours,**" Matt told Alison.

Parts of speech

Verb: A **verb** shows an action or a state of being in a sentence. To help you decide whether a word is a verb, ask *Does it show what happens (action)?* or *Does it show what is (state of being)?*

> Matt **said,** "You always **wear** that hat." Alison **answered,** "Yes, it **is** my favorite, but I **will wear** my other hat tomorrow."

Verbs also have **tenses.** Tenses tell when the action takes place.

Irregular Verbs	
Present	**Past**
break	broke
go	went
know	knew
say	said
think	thought
write	wrote

- Past tense shows that the action has already happened. **Regular** verbs form the past tense by adding *–ed.* **Irregular** verbs form the past tense differently. The chart shows some irregular verbs.
- Present tense shows that the action happens often or is happening now.
- Future tense shows that the action will happen. In the sentence above, <u>will wear</u> is in the future tense.

Adjective: An **adjective** tells how a noun or pronoun looks, acts, sounds, smells, tastes, or feels. To help you decide whether a word is an adjective, ask *What kind?, Which one?,* or *How many?*

> Matt wore his **old brown** jacket.

The words <u>a</u>, <u>an</u>, and <u>the</u> are special adjectives called **articles.**

Adverb: An **adverb** tells about a verb, an adjective, or another adverb. To help you decide whether a word is an adverb, ask *When?, Where?, How?,* or *How much?*

> Matt skied **quickly** down the hill.
> The mountain was **very** beautiful.

Preposition: A **preposition** shows how two parts of a sentence are related, or tied to one another. Some prepositions are <u>to</u>, <u>with</u>, <u>out</u>, <u>over</u>, <u>near</u>, <u>across</u>, <u>in</u>, <u>of</u>, <u>under</u>, <u>before</u>, and <u>along</u>. Nouns or pronouns follow prepositions. The combination of a preposition, a noun or a pronoun, and the words between them is called a **prepositional phrase.**

> He came **from** the market. She climbed **over** the mountain.

Conjunction: A **conjunction** joins words or ideas. Common conjunctions are <u>and</u>, <u>or</u>, <u>but</u>, and <u>so</u>.

> Alison **and** Matt skied all day, **but** they never fell.

◼ Use It

Read the passage. Decide what part of speech each word is.

Yesterday was a warm spring day. Martin and I drank raindrops. He jumped high in deep puddles. He got his shoes muddy. We ran quickly and skipped through his large garden on the wet path.

Look at the chart. Fill in the blanks with words from the passage. Write each word next to its correct part of speech.

Part of Speech	Words
Noun	day, Martin, _____, _____, _____, garden, _____
Pronoun	I, He, He, _____, _____, _____
Verb	was, drank, jumped, _____, _____, _____
Adjective	a, warm, spring, deep, _____, _____, the, _____
Adverb	Yesterday, high, _____
Preposition	in, _____, _____
Conjunction	_____, _____

Read the passage. Look at the <u>underlined</u> verbs. Then fill in the chart below.

"Abby, your room <u>is</u> a mess. Please <u>clean</u> it up," <u>said</u> Abby's mother.

Abby <u>looked</u> at the toys and clothes on the floor. "Maybe my mother is right," Abby <u>thought</u>. "I <u>will clean</u> this up tonight."

Verb	Tense
is	
clean	
said	past
looked	
thought	
will clean	

Practice It

Read each item. Circle the letter of the correct answer.

1. | John wrote a long letter to Lia and <u>me</u>. |

   The <u>underlined</u> word is a —

   A noun

   B pronoun

   C adjective

   D verb

2. | He hid <u>under</u> his bed during the game of hide and seek. |

   The <u>underlined</u> word is a —

   A pronoun

   B adjective

   C verb

   D preposition

3. **Which word below is an irregular verb?**

   A jumped

   B talked

   C guessed

   D brought

4. **Which word below is a preposition?**

   A she

   B talk

   C in

   D quickly

 Tip Ask questions to help you find a word's part of speech.

Subjects and Verbs Agree

◼ Study It

How do you know which verb to use in a sentence? It depends on the subject of the sentence. The subject tells <u>who</u> or <u>what</u> the sentence is about. Subjects are usually nouns or pronouns.

The subject and verb must always agree in number.

- A singular subject is one person, place, or thing. A singular subject takes a singular verb. The pronouns <u>he</u>, <u>she</u>, and <u>it</u> are also singular subjects.

    Jonathan likes his new sweater. **It looks** comfortable.

    Are you going swimming?

<u>You</u> can be singular or plural. Sometimes <u>you</u> is a group of people. At other times, <u>you</u> is one person.

- A plural subject is more than one person, place, or thing. A plural subject takes a plural verb. The pronouns <u>we</u>, <u>you</u>, and <u>they</u> are also plural subjects.

    The **boys paddle** the canoe. **They prepare** the meals.

Subjects and verbs agree even when other words come between them. Watch for **compound subjects,** two or more subjects joined by a conjunction. Compound subjects joined by <u>and</u> need a plural verb.

    Jonathan and Keesha like lemonade.

    Greg and his sisters sing in the play.

<u>Jonathan and Keesha</u> is a compound subject. The verb <u>like</u> is a plural verb. The subject of the second sentence is <u>Greg and his sisters</u>. This is also a compound subject, so the verb <u>sing</u> is plural.

Subjects and verbs must also agree when the verb comes before the subject.

    On the desk **are** two **pencils.**

The verb <u>are</u> comes before the subject <u>pencils</u>. The subject is plural, so the verb <u>are</u> agrees with the subject.

Subject-verb agreement

Use It

The subject and the verb in each sentence are <u>underlined</u>. If the subject and verb <u>agree</u>, write agree in the blank. If they do not agree, write the correct verb in the blank. Look at these examples.

_____agree_____ 1. The <u>firefighter</u> <u>hooks</u> the ladder to the fire truck.

_____are_____ 2. A <u>whale and a seal</u> <u>is</u> two animals that swim.

Now you try it.

_____ 1. <u>Greg</u>, like his sisters, <u>want</u> to see the movie.

_____ 2. <u>Is</u> <u>Nina and Isa</u> ready to go?

_____ 3. <u>She</u> <u>has</u> a green notebook.

Practice It

Read each sentence. Choose the answer that will correct the <u>underlined</u> words. Circle the letter of the correct answer.

1. | The <u>train</u> <u>pull</u> into the station early in the morning. |

   A trains pulls

   B train pulls

   C train are pulling

   D correct as is

2. | The <u>flag</u> <u>flap</u> in the breeze. |

   A flag are flapping

   B flags flaps

   C flags flap

   D correct as is

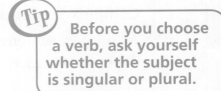

Tip
Before you choose a verb, ask yourself whether the subject is singular or plural.

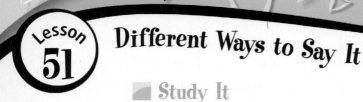

Different Ways to Say It

Study It

Using different types of sentences keeps readers interested. Careful use of punctuation and language helps readers understand how ideas in a sentence work together.

Look at the chart. It shows three different kinds of sentences.

Sentence Type	Example
Simple	Antoine's dog is friendly.
Compound	Antoine's dog is friendly, and he likes to play.
Complex	Antoine's friendly dog wags his tail when I visit.

Basic Sentence Parts

An **independent clause** is a group of words that is a complete thought. It has a subject and a predicate. An independent clause is a sentence.

Jane learned about elephants.

A **dependent clause** is a group of words that has a subject and predicate, but it is not a sentence. A dependent clause may also be called a **subordinate clause.**

After they swam in the lake, Frederick and Jamal were tired.

Types of Sentences

Simple Sentence

A simple sentence is an independent clause.

Baseball is a game.   Birds flew across the sky.

Compound Sentence

A compound sentence is a sentence made up of two or more independent clauses joined by a comma and a conjunction such as <u>and</u>, <u>or</u>, <u>but</u>, and <u>so</u>.

My aunt fixed lunch, and I set the table.

Complex Sentence

A complex sentence has one independent clause and at least one dependent clause.

When Mary reached the corner, she turned left.
OR Mary turned left when she reached the corner.

Sentence types

Use It

**Read the sentences. Write <u>compound</u> or <u>complex</u> on the line.
Look at these examples.**

_____complex_____ 1. After I ate my lunch, I took a nap.

_____compound_____ 2. It was raining, but the sun shone brightly.

Now you try it.

_____ 1. When I dropped my pencil, the tip broke.

_____ 2. Ana left the birthday party, but I stayed to help clean up.

_____ 3. We can walk, or we can ride the bus.

_____ 4. I always wash my hands before I eat.

Practice It

Read the items. Circle the letter of the correct answer.

1. **Which of the following is a dependent clause?**

   A When the summer season ends.

   B We sailed and landed on a tiny island.

   C He had a snack after lunch.

   D She painted the name on the boat.

2. **Which sentence is a complex sentence?**

   A Gil brushed the horse's mane, and Betsy cleaned the stable.

   B Sal loved picking blueberries when she came to visit.

   C Isabella mowed the lawn last week.

   D They pulled the red wagon behind them.

Tip
To find the sentence type, look for independent and dependent clauses.

The Busy Comma

Study It

Commas set apart words or phrases within a sentence. They also separate parts of dates and addresses.

Here are some common uses for the comma.

- Use a comma to separate two independent clauses in a compound sentence.

    Mike took the bus, but Isabel drove her car.

- Use a comma to set off a dependent clause when it is the first part of a complex sentence.

    When Ali came up to bat, she hit a home run.

- Use a comma to set off an **appositive phrase.** An appositive phrase is a noun or phrase that explains another noun. Appositives are not necessary to the meaning of the sentence. Sentence with appositive: George, **my cousin,** is moving.

- Use a comma in a list of three or more items.

    We saw **bears, tigers,** and **monkeys** at the zoo last week.

    He **cleared the table, washed the dishes,** and **swept the floor.**

- Use a comma to set off the name of a person being spoken to.

    Dwayne, can you come here? I don't think so, **Stephanie.**

- Use a comma to set off words such as <u>yes</u>, <u>no</u>, and <u>well</u> at the beginning of a sentence.

    No, I can't go to the meeting. **Yes,** I'll call you later.

- Use a comma to separate the day of the month from the year. Place a comma after the year when other words follow in the sentence.

    Maria was born **April 2, 1998,** in New York.

- Use a comma to separate the name of a city from the name of a state or country. Place a comma after a state or country when other words follow in the sentence.

    Didn't he move here from **Nome, Alaska,** last fall?

Use It

Read each sentence. Rewrite each sentence on the line, with commas in the correct places. Look at these examples.

1. He was born in Springfield Vermont in 1864.
   He was born in Springfield, Vermont, in 1864.

2. Yes I will be glad to take her with me.
   Yes, I will be glad to take her with me.

Now you try it.

1. Vicente washed the car raked the leaves and took a nap.

   _____

2. Mrs. Ruiz our neighbor baked a cake for us.

   _____

Practice It

Read each sentence. Choose the answer that will correct the underlined part of the sentence. Circle the letter of the correct answer.

1. My <u>cat a tabby</u> is just six months old.

   A cat a tabby,

   B cat, a tabby

   C cat, a tabby,

   D correct as is

Tip Commas make sentences easier to understand.

2. Mattie <u>cleaned the bathroom swept the rug and folded the clothes.</u>

   A ,cleaned the bathroom, swept the rug and folded the clothes

   B cleaned the bathroom, swept the rug, and folded the clothes

   C cleaned the bathroom swept the rug, and folded the clothes

   D correct as is

Signs and Rules

Study It

Using punctuation marks correctly makes sentences easier to understand. Parentheses, quotation marks, and apostrophes are all types of punctuation. It is also important to use underlining correctly.

To add an explanation to a sentence, use **parentheses** ( ).

The school play will be held next Thursday (the second Thursday of the month).

To tell readers that you are using a **direct quotation,** use **quotation marks (" ").** A direct quotation is someone's exact words. Use a comma before the quotation marks of a direct quotation. At the end of the quotation, add a comma if the sentence does not end with the quotation. Add a final punctuation mark if the sentence does end with the quotation. Then close the quotation marks.

Father said, "Everyone needs to get in the car."

"When will you go," asked Chris, "and when will you come back?"

To help the reader understand titles, use **underlining** (italics if you are using a computer) or quotation marks. Underline the titles of books, plays, magazines, films, and works of art. Use quotation marks for the titles of stories, songs, and poems.

Wilbur is a character in Charlotte's Web.
OR Wilbur is a character in *Charlotte's Web.*

The song "The Circle of Life" is from the movie The Lion King.

In a **contraction,** a word made from two words, an **apostrophe** (') takes the place of letters that have been left out.

Norma **can't** come to the party.

Apostrophes also show ownership or **possession.** To make a singular noun possessive, add *'s.* To make most plural nouns possessive, add only an apostrophe after the *s.* If a plural does not end in *s,* add *'s.*

Singular noun: **Lisa's** dog is friendly.
Plural noun: The **boys'** team won.
Plural noun: The **men's** hats are black.

Punctuation

Use It

Rewrite each sentence on the line, using correct punctuation.
Look at these examples.

1. Jan asked How many people are coming to the cookout?
Jan asked, "How many people are coming to the cookout?"

2. We sang Row, Row, Row Your Boat at the cookout.
We sang "Row, Row, Row Your Boat" at the cookout.

Now you try it.

1. Did you fill Sparkys water dish?

   _____

2. Rita cant find her spelling book.

   _____

3. That paper is mine Carlos said.

   _____

Practice It

Read each sentence. Choose the answer that shows the correct punctuation. Circle the letter of the correct answer.

1. **I dont see how we can all fit in that car said Rick.**

   A I dont see how we can all fit in that car, said Rick

   B "I don't see how we can all fit in that car said Rick."

   C "I don't see how we can all fit in that car," said Rick.

   D correct as is

2. **Robert Jones is the author of ten childrens books.**

   A "Robert Jones" is the author of ten children's books.

   B Robert Jones is the author of ten children's books.

   C Robert Jones is the author of ten children's books.

   D correct as is

 Tip When using quotation marks, find the exact words of the speaker.

Standing Tall

Lesson 54

Study It

Capital letters, or uppercase letters, always begin the first word in a sentence and the first word of a direct quotation.

Nouns that name a person, place, or thing, such as city, are called **common nouns.** Nouns that name a particular person, place, or thing, such as Dallas, are called **proper nouns.** Each word of a proper noun begins with a capital letter.

Look at these examples of common and proper nouns.

Type of Noun	Common Nouns	Proper (or special) Nouns
Person	aunt	**Aunt Sally**
	boy	**Jim**
	teacher	**Mr. Simms**
Place	city, state	**Tampa, Florida**
	country	the **United States of America**
	mountain	**Mount Washington**
Thing	month	**May**
	holiday	**Thanksgiving**
	club	**Girl Scouts**
	building	the **Sears Tower**

Here are three rules for capitalizing the **titles** of books, magazines, organizations (groups), works of art, music, and movies.

- Capitalize the first word of the title.
- Capitalize all important words.
- Capitalize forms of the verb be.

Do not capitalize these words unless they begin a title.

- the articles a, an, and the
- conjunctions, such as and, but, or, and so
- prepositions that have fewer than five letters, such as with and for

Use It

Rewrite each sentence on the line, using correct capitalization. Look at this example.

She wanted to know whether hector had read a Book called *The Mouse Went To the City.*

She wanted to know whether Hector had read a book *called The Mouse Went to the City.*

Now you try it.

1. During thanksgiving vacation, I traveled with my family to new york.

_____

_____

2. My sister saw the empire state building for the first time. She said, "it is taller than I thought it would be."

_____

_____

Practice It

Read each sentence. Choose the answer that shows correct capitalization. Circle the letter of the correct answer.

1. **He asked, "are we going to Lake Louise?"**

   A He asked, "are we going to lake louise?"

   B He asked, "are we going to lake Louise?"

   C He asked, "Are we going to Lake Louise?"

   D correct as is

2. **We saw the painting *sunflowers* at the museum.**

   A We saw the painting *Sunflowers* at the museum.

   B We saw the painting *sunflowers* at the Museum.

   C We saw the Painting *sunflowers* at the museum.

   D correct as is

Tip Make sure that each proper noun begins with a capital letter.

Unit 10
Test-Taking Strategy

Strategy: Toss and Match

In this unit you learned that language follows rules. Use these steps to answer test items that ask you to correct sentences.

- Read the sentence. Then read each answer choice carefully. Think about the language rules. Toss out the answers that you know break the language rules.

- If you are not sure which of the remaining answers is the correct one, think about how you would rewrite the sentence.

- Look for the answer choice that matches your rewrite.

Try It Out
Read the item. Circle the letter of the correct answer.

Ellie Anna and Trevor are in the big show.

Which sentence uses commas correctly?

A   Ellie, Anna, and Trevor, are in the big show.

B   Ellie, Anna, and, Trevor are in the big show.

C   Ellie, Anna, and Trevor are in the big show.

D   correct as is

Read the sentence. Then read the answer choices. Which ones have mistakes? Toss them out. In this item, the sentence is hard to understand without commas. Toss out answer choice **D** because the answer is not correct as is. Answer choice **A** is incorrect. No rule says to put a comma before the verb. Answer choice **B** is incorrect. No rule says to put a comma after the conjunction <u>and</u>. Answer choice **C** uses commas in a list of three or more people. Answer choice **C** is correct.

Put It to the Test

Name _____

This test will check what you have learned in this unit.

DIRECTIONS: Circle the letter of the correct answer.

1. | Pack your gloves hat and sweater |

   What is the correct punctuation for this sentence?

   A Pack your gloves, hat and, sweater.

   B Pack your gloves, hat, and sweater.

   C Pack your gloves hat, and sweater

   D correct as is

2. | The child rode her scooter. |

   The nouns in this sentence are —

   A child, scooter

   B child, rode

   C rode, her

   D her, scooter

3. **What is the correct way to write the title of a book?**

   A the Dragon nanny

   B "The Dragon nanny"

   C *The Dragon Nanny*

   D (The Dragon Nanny)

4. | The students talked over their plan. |

   The pronoun in this sentence is —

   A students

   B talked

   C their

   D plan

5. **Which sentence is in the past tense?**

   A The trumpets announce the king.

   B The trumpets are announcing the king.

   C The trumpets will announce the king.

   D The trumpets announced the king.

6. | Mr. Wilson was at the wrong house. |

   The verb in this sentence is —

   A wrong

   B was

   C at

   D house

GO ON

Achieve It! Practice Cards

_____

7. | After we started the fire, we cooked the fish.

This is an example of a —

A simple sentence

B compound sentence

C complex sentence

D sentence with an appositive

8. Which sentence is correct?

A He and I is leaving now.

B He and I are leaving now.

C He and I am leaving now.

D He and I was leaving now.

9. | She <u>bringed</u> the parrot to Lisa's house.

The correct verb is —

A bringing

B brought

C branged

D correct as is

10. Which sentence is correct?

A "Which way, asked Monica, is the shoe repair shop"

B Which way, asked Monica, is the shoe repair shop?

C "Which way," asked Monica, "is the shoe repair shop?"

D "Which way?" asked Monica, "is the shoe repair shop."

11. | Jan was born on July 7 1996.

What is the correct punctuation for this sentence?

A Jan was born on July, 7 1996.

B Jan was born on, July 7, 1996.

C Jan was born on July 7, 1996.

D correct as is

12. | On friday they played in Settlers' park.

What is the correct capitalization for this sentence?

A On Friday they played in Settlers' Park.

B On friday they played in Settlers' Park.

C On Friday they played in settlers' park.

D correct as is

13. | Dr. Ree my doctor is busy now.

What is the correct way to write this sentence?

A Dr. Ree my doctor is, busy, now.

B Dr. Ree my doctor, is busy now.

C Dr. Ree, my doctor, is busy now.

D correct as is

STOP

Achieve It! Practice Cards

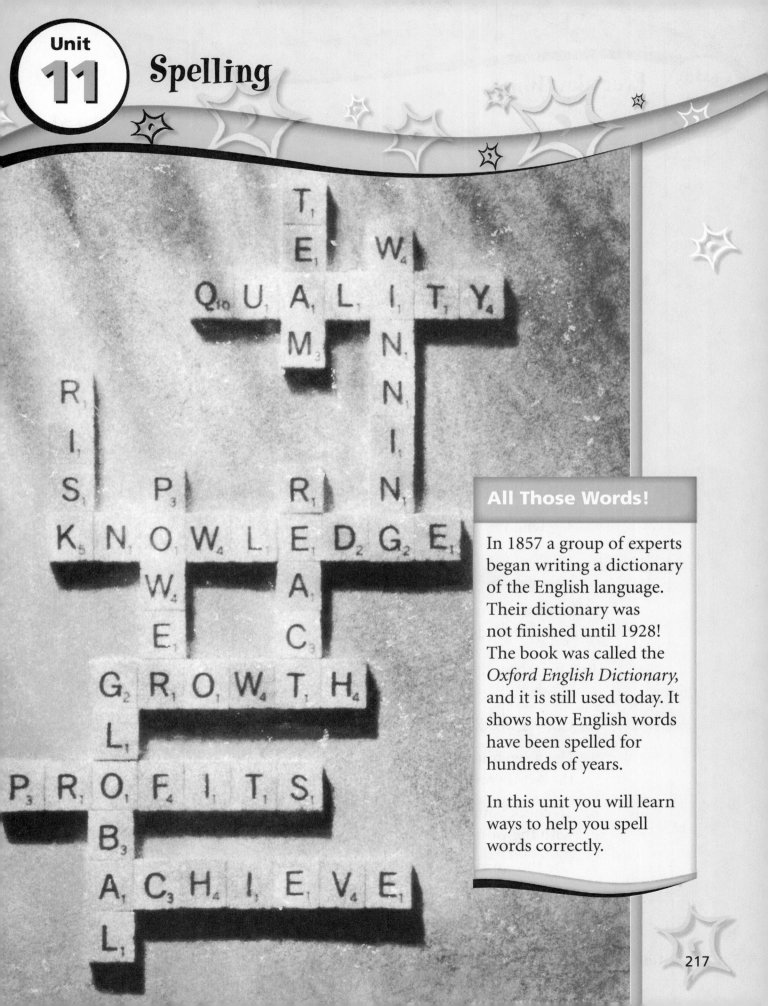

All Those Words!

In 1857 a group of experts began writing a dictionary of the English language. Their dictionary was not finished until 1928! The book was called the *Oxford English Dictionary,* and it is still used today. It shows how English words have been spelled for hundreds of years.

In this unit you will learn ways to help you spell words correctly.

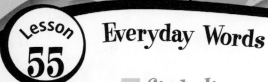

Everyday Words

▪ Study It

It is important to know how to spell the words that you write.

Look at this chart. It shows some words that are used often. Notice the spelling of each word.

Words You Use Often		
• when	• since	• clothes
• here	• there	• might
• which	• their	• whole
• been	• write	• many

Now look at this chart. It shows a way you can practice spelling words correctly.

Column 1	Column 2	Column 3
WORD	**WRITE**	**SENTENCE**
when	when	When can we meet to practice our spelling?

Make a list of words that you use often. You can spell words more easily if you study them in this way.

1. On a sheet of paper, draw a three-column chart like the one above.

2. Copy a word that you want to learn to spell in Column 1.

3. Use a separate sheet of paper to cover Column 1. Think about the word you copied. Write it in Column 2.

4. To check your spelling, compare the word you wrote in Column 2 with the word in Column 1. The two spellings should match.

5. Use the word in a sentence in Column 3.

High frequency words

Use It

Fill in the empty spaces in the chart below. Use a sheet of paper to hide the word in Column 1 when you write in Columns 2 and 3.

| Column 1 | Column 2 | Column 3 |
WORD	WRITE	SENTENCE
maybe	maybe	Maybe we can feed the goldfish today.
been	been	We have been to the state fair!

Now you try it.

| Column 1 | Column 2 | Column 3 |
WORD	WRITE	SENTENCE
which		
their		

Practice It

Choose the correct spelling for each missing word. Circle the letter of the correct answer.

1. **We bought _____ to make toast.**

   A bredd

   B bread

   C brid

   D brede

2. **The pieces fit _____.**

   A toogethr

   B twogether

   C together

   D togeter

Tip

When you spell a word incorrectly, add the correct spelling of that word to your spelling chart.

Looking at Word Parts

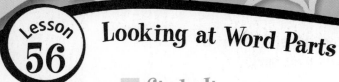

Study It

The **root** of a word is the main part of the word. Sometimes you will need to change the spelling of a root word to add an ending. These rules can help you remember how to add parts to root words.

Final *e* Rule When a word ends in a silent *e*, drop the *e* before adding *-ing* or *-ed*.

fade fad~~e~~ + ed = faded   **glide** glid~~e~~ + ing = gliding

Doubling Rule When a one-syllable word ends in a consonant-vowel-consonant pattern (CVC), such as t<u>ra</u>p, double the final consonant before adding *-ing* or *-ed*.

tip tip + p + ed = tipped   **fit** fit + t + ing = fitting

Other words have more than one syllable, such as <u>admit</u>. When a word with two or more syllables ends in a CVC pattern, double the last consonant only if the final syllable is stressed.

In the word <u>admit</u>, the final syllable *mit* is stressed, so the last consonant is doubled.

admit admit + t + ed = admitted

In the word <u>quiver</u>, the final syllable <u>er</u> is not stressed, so the last consonant is not doubled.

quiver quiver + ing = quivering

Plural Rule To make most nouns plural, add an *s*. For words ending in *s, x, ch,* or *sh,* add *es.*

<u>table</u> + s = tables   <u>fox</u> + es = foxes

<u>success</u> + es = successes   <u>crash</u> + es = crashes

***y* to *i* Rule** To make a noun plural when the final two letters are a consonant and *y*, change the *y* to *i* and add *es.*

butterfly butterfl~~y~~ + i + es = butterflies

Structural analysis

◣ **Use It**

Spell each underlined word correctly. Look at these examples.

<u>swimming</u> 1. I was <u>swiming</u> in the pool.

<u>shivered</u> 2. The dog <u>shiverred</u> in the cold.

Now you try it.

_____ 1. They were <u>paddleing</u> down the river.

_____ 2. We bought three <u>bunchs</u> of grapes.

_____ 3. We saw ripe <u>cherrys</u> on the tree.

_____ 4. They were <u>claping</u> about the ending.

◣ **Practice It**

Choose the correct spelling for each missing word. Circle the letter of the correct answer.

1. We _____ through the gate.

   A enteried

   B enterred

   C entered

   D enterd

2. **Three students gave _____ .**

   A speeches

   B speches

   C speechs

   D spechs

3. **The _____ of the story was very interesting.**

   A begining

   B beginning

   C begininng

   D beginiing

Tip
Spell out long words one syllable at a time, and look at each word part.

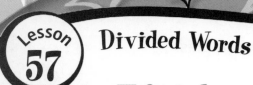

Divided Words

◢ Study It

Syllables

A **syllable** is a word or part of a word that can be pronounced by itself, such as <u>fa</u> in <u>father</u>. A syllable contains only one vowel sound.

Learning to spell a word one syllable at a time can help you spell the whole word correctly. Here are some rules to help you divide words into syllables.

-le **Rule** If a word ends in a consonant and *-le,* it is divided before the consonant that comes before *-le.*

jun • gle   rid • dle   han • dle

Open Syllable Rule An **open syllable** is one that ends in a vowel. The vowel usually has a long sound and says its name. Divide the word after the first vowel. For example, the syllable <u>ba</u> in <u>bacon</u> is an open syllable. It has a long ā sound.

ba • con   o • pen   cra • zy   pi • rate

Closed Syllable Rule A **closed syllable** follows the pattern of consonant-vowel-consonant (CVC). In a closed syllable, the vowel has a short sound. Divide the word after the closed syllable.

six • teen   blos • som   res • cue

cos • tume   gal • lop   lum • ber

You can divide a word into syllables to make spelling the word easier. Use the same rules to divide a long word that you use to divide a short one. Check your work by looking up the words in a dictionary. The dictionary shows you the correct spelling and how the word is divided into syllables.

Syllabic rules

Use It

Divide these words into syllables. Then write which rule you are using. Look at these examples.

1. paddle   pad • dle; -*le* rule

2. problem   prob • lem; closed syllable rule

Now you try it.

1. protect   _____

2. mention   _____

3. preserve   _____

4. giggle   _____

Practice It

Choose the correct spelling for each missing word. Circle the letter of the correct answer.

1. **Which is the correct way to divide the word <u>marble</u> into syllables?**

    A ma • rble

    B marb • le

    C mar • ble

    D marbl • e

2. **Which is the correct way to divide the word <u>nature</u> into syllables?**

    A nat • ure

    B na • ture

    C natu • re

    D nature

Tip   **Each syllable has one "beat." Count syllables by clapping your hands as you say a word.**

Unit 11
Test-Taking Strategy

Strategy: Be Prepared

In this unit you have learned spelling rules. Here are some tips to help you spell words correctly.

- Make a list of words you use often, and learn their spellings.
- Know that different letters make different sounds.
- Look closely at the differences between homophones, such as their and there, which sound the same but are spelled differently.
- Look at word parts, such as syllables and endings.
- Remember the rules for adding endings to words.
- Remember the rules for dividing words into syllables.

Try It Out

Read this sentence carefully. Think about the spelling rules you have learned.

Choose the word that is spelled correctly. Circle the letter of the correct answer.

Our class is cleaning up the park. Our _____ are painting and sweeping.

A dutys

B dutyies

C duties

D dutties

The word duty ends in a consonant and y. You must follow the y to i rule to make this word plural. Change the y to i and add es. The correct answer is **C.**

Unit 11 • Spelling
Put It to the Test

This test will check what you have learned in this unit.

DIRECTIONS: Circle the letter of the correct answer.

1. The weather is _____ cold.

   A geting

   B getting

   C gedding

   D getinng

2. The horses are _____ in the parade.

   A prancing

   B pranceing

   C pranccing

   D prancceing

3. Add two _____ of salt to the vegetables.

   A pinchs

   B pinchess

   C pinchz

   D pinches

4. Which is the correct way to divide the word <u>demand</u> into syllables?

   A de • mand

   B dem • and

   C dema • nd

   D deman • d

5. We went to a farm to pick _____ last week.

   A berrys

   B berryes

   C berries

   D berrees

6. The boy ate the _____ apple.

   A houl

   B whole

   C hole

   D whol

7. They _____ the lights as the movie began.

   A dimed

   B dimmed

   C dimd

   D dimmied

GO ON

Achieve It! Practice Cards

_____

8. Which is the correct way to divide the word <u>control</u> into syllables?

   A co • ntrol

   B cont • rol

   C con • trol

   D contr • ol

9. The girls _____ about the cat in the tree until it was rescued.

   A worried

   B woried

   C worryed

   D woryed

10. His mother's _____ gave prizes at our school carnival.

    A busness

    B business

    C bisness

    D busines

11. We _____ to help the team win the game.

    A tryed

    B tryyed

    C triad

    D tried

12. Which is the correct way to divide the word <u>twenty</u> into syllables?

    A twen • ty

    B twent • y

    C twe • nty

    D tw • enty

13. Do not fall and _____ yourself.

    A hurte

    B heart

    C hert

    D hurt

14. The new _____ are hiring workers next week.

    A factoryies

    B factories

    C factorys

    D factorries

15. Which is the correct way to divide the word <u>person</u> into syllables?

    A pe • rson

    B per • son

    C pers • on

    D perso • n

STOP

Achieve It! Practice Cards

_____

Practice Test A

Here are a few tips to keep in mind when you take a test:

- Read all directions and test items carefully.
- Read each answer choice carefully.
- Choose the best answer.

Complete this sample to help you get ready to take this practice test.

SAMPLE

DIRECTIONS: Read the item. Circle the letter of the correct answer.

> **Vincent got a running start before he <u>bounded</u> across the puddle.**
>
> **What does the word <u>bounded</u> mean in this sentence?**
>
> **A** strolled
>
> **B** swam
>
> **C** jumped
>
> **D** crawled
>
> The correct answer is **C.** The word <u>bounded</u> means "jumped." Circle the letter **C.**

Some parts of this test will have passages for you to read. Read each passage carefully. Then answer the questions about the passage.

DIRECTIONS: Read each item. Circle the letter of the correct answer on your _Achieve It!_ Practice Test Answer Sheet.

1. | Keep your answers as short as possible, and do not add any <u>unnecessary</u> words.

If <u>necessary</u> means "needed," what does <u>unnecessary</u> mean?

A   less needed

B   needed a bit

C   not needed

D   needed more

2. | We tried to <u>observe</u> the game carefully so we would know how to play it.

What does the word <u>observe</u> mean in this sentence?

A   watch

B   count

C   photograph

D   list

3. | After dinner I have several <u>chores</u>, such as clearing the table and washing the dishes.

Which word means the SAME as <u>chores</u>?

A   experiments

B   loads

C   objects

D   duties

4. | We got to school late because we were caught in a huge traffic <u>jam</u>.

jam (jam) **_n._ 1** a sweet food made from fruit and sugar **2** people or cars crowded and unable to move **_v._ 3** to get stuck and not work **4** to squeeze things into a small place

Which meaning BEST fits the way <u>jam</u> is used in this sentence?

A   meaning 1

B   meaning 2

C   meaning 3

D   meaning 4

5. | I looked at the map, but I could not <u>locate</u> your street.

Which word means the SAME as <u>locate</u>?

A   find

B   walk

C   admire

D   spell

GO ON

6. The farmers are expecting a big corn <u>crop</u> this year.

crop (krop) *n.* **1** the amount of a food that is picked at one harvest **2** part of a bird's body where food is stored **3** things that appear at the same time, as in "a crop of problems" *v.* **4** to cut off

Which meaning BEST fits the way <u>crop</u> is used in this sentence?

A   meaning 1

B   meaning 2

C   meaning 3

D   meaning 4

7. When I saw an elephant at the zoo, I was surprised at how <u>enormous</u> it looked next to a zebra.

Which word means the OPPOSITE of <u>enormous</u>?

A   useful

B   lively

C   eager

D   small

8. We gave the author a pen so that she could <u>autograph</u> her picture in our books.

What does the word <u>autograph</u> mean in this sentence?

A   sign

B   approve

C   buy

D   deliver

9. When the ant farm fell to the floor, it took me several hours to <u>recapture</u> the ants.

If <u>capture</u> means "catch," what does <u>recapture</u> mean?

A   catch inside

B   catch again

C   catch later

D   catch before

10. The teacher will <u>demonstrate</u> the correct way to turn on the computer so we can do it on our own.

What does the word <u>demonstrate</u> mean in this sentence?

A   examine

B   watch

C   show

D   understand

GO ON

Kira's Stuff

"Kiirrraaa! What is THIS?" Kira's mother, standing next to the washing machine, held up a pair of tattered jeans. "You haven't worn these since you were seven!"

Kira sighed and reached for the jeans. "I know. I didn't want to throw them out. I wore them at the family picnic where I met Susie."

On that day Kira had bumped into Susie as she was getting cold drinks. As the girls said they were sorry to each other, Kira's Aunt Margo hurried up and reached for a diet soda.

"Hi, Kira, I'm glad you're here. Have you two met?" Without waiting for an answer, she continued, "It's too bad you live so far apart. Susie is so sweet. Do you know what her first spoken sentence was?"

Susie rolled her eyes as Aunt Margo continued. "She said, 'I have a collection.' Isn't that cute? Do you collect anything, Kira?" Before Kira could answer, Aunt Margo hurried off, shouting, "You girls go talk!" over her shoulder.

The girls moved over to a picnic bench far away from the smoking barbecue grill. Carefully, Susie placed her basket on the table.

"Is that your lunch?" Kira asked.

"Nope. It's one of those collections Aunt Margo mentioned." Susie reached into the basket and pulled out a tan rock with sharp edges. "See the little bits that shine in the sunlight like diamonds? I found this one day when I was walking home from school. Mom was with me, and I'd had a bad day. I looked down and saw this rock. Mom said it was like life—rough, sharp, but full of diamonds if you just looked. I thought that was kind of neat."

One by one, Susie took out the rocks from her basket. Each rock had a special story.

"Kira," her mother said sharply, bringing her back to the present, "I asked you about these jeans."

"I want to keep them," Kira said firmly, carefully folding the jeans into a small square. "They got in the wash by mistake."

Kira's mother shook her head, picked up the laundry basket, and headed into the kitchen. "I don't even WANT to know what else you've squirreled away," she added.

Kira groaned quietly and went into her room. She pulled an old suitcase out from the back of her closet and lifted it onto the bed. Inside was a jumble of objects. Carefully, she began to arrange the objects so that she could tuck the jeans in among them.

"Kiirrrraaa!" Kira hurried out of her room and down the hall.

Mrs. Cortinez and her daughter Christina were standing in the hallway. "Your Mom and I are working on things for the craft fair," she said to Kira. "Why don't you girls go study?"

Kira sighed and led the way to her room. "I suppose we could clear off the bed. . . ." Horrified, she realized that she had left her suitcase out—and open! Christina would tell everyone at school, and they'd never stop laughing!

"What's this?" Christina headed for the bed like a homing pigeon.

"Nothing." Kira tried to move between Christina and the suitcase, but she wasn't fast enough.

"Oooh, this is a cool necklace." Christina held up a string of purple plastic beads. "Where'd you get it?"

"Please, let me put that away, and we'll study."

Christina reached into the suitcase again and pulled out a soft piece of pink fabric. "What's this? It's really pretty."

"It's part of my baby blanket. My aunt made it for me before I was born."

"You're lucky to have this stuff," Christina said.

One by one, Christina took things out of the suitcase, and Kira told her the story about each object. Soon, bits and pieces of fabric, ribbons, beads, photographs, pictures, and dried flowers littered Kira's bed.

GO ON

"Kiiirrrraa!"

"Quick, get this stuff into the suitcase!" Kira began grabbing things and stuffing them quickly into the suitcase.

But not quite fast enough. Kira's mother stood in the doorway, staring at the room in dismay. Mrs. Cortinez peered over her shoulder.

"Look!" Christina held out a scrap of purple silk. "This is from an old dress Kira's grandma wore, and this. . . ."

"Kira! What IS all this?" her mother demanded.

Kira hung her head sadly. "Just stuff," she mumbled. "I'll get rid of it."

"No!" Christina protested. "This stuff is important to you."

Mrs. Cortinez nodded. "You must keep what's important where you can see it."

"Betty," Kira's mother said sternly to Mrs. Cortinez, "she can't leave them all out in her room. Look at the mess."

"Oh, I think she CAN leave them out. I have an idea. Christina, help carry Kira's things into the kitchen."

They spent the next few hours sewing and gluing Kira's stuff to a big piece of cloth. Kira's baby blanket was sewn onto the upper right corner and was covered partway by the purple fabric. Across that, the beads were glued in place as well as an old veil taken from a favorite hat of Kira's great grandmother. Kira's "stuff" completely covered the fabric.

"Now," Mrs. Cortinez announced, "we'll put a broom handle through the top, tie ribbons onto the ends of the handle, and hang this on the wall. You'll have all your stuff, Kira, and your wall will be beautiful."

Kira's mother looked at their work and nodded. "That works. That actually works!" She smiled.

Mrs. Corintez added, "Your stuff is full of memories, Kira. Those memories are stories that should be told and remembered!"

11. **How does meeting Susie change Kira?**

   A   She becomes interested in collecting rocks.

   B   She wants to go to more craft fairs.

   C   She recognizes that she should not keep her old jeans.

   D   She realizes how important it is to remember special stories.

12. **Mrs. Cortinez is DIFFERENT from Kira's mother because —**

   A   Mrs. Cortinez likes working at the craft fair

   B   Mrs. Cortinez thinks Kira's stuff is important

   C   Mrs. Cortinez wants Kira to be neat

   D   Mrs. Cortinez thinks Kira is unkind

13. **What happens AFTER Christina finds the suitcase?**

   A   The girls pull out the old clothes and dress up.

   B   The girls begin to study for a test.

   C   Kira's stuff gets scattered across her bed.

   D   Kira hides the suitcase in the closet.

14. **What is the MAIN problem in the story?**

   A   Kira's mother thinks Kira does not study enough.

   B   Kira's mother is unhappy because Kira hides things in the basement.

   C   Kira's mother thinks Kira's room is not neat and tidy.

   D   Kira's mother thinks Kira's special things make a mess.

15. **Kira keeps her stuff in a suitcase because —**

   A   it is special and she doesn't want to throw it away

   B   that is where Susie kept her special things

   C   she is planning on visiting Susie very soon

   D   it helps her carry her things around with her

16. **What is the MAIN message of the story?**

   A   Everyone should collect something.

   B   A messy room will always get you in trouble.

   C   Memories of special things are important.

   D   Save everything from your childhood.

GO ON

17. **Where do Kira and Susie meet?**

    A   at a fair

    B   at school

    C   at a picnic

    D   at a house

18. **Which phrase from the story is a simile?**

    A   away from the smoking barbecue grill

    B   shine in the sunlight like diamonds

    C   sharp, but full of diamonds

    D   those memories are stories

19. **Why does Kira want to hide the suitcase before Christina sees it?**

    A   She is afraid that Christina will make fun of her.

    B   She thinks Christina will take her stuff.

    C   She does not like to share her special memories.

    D   She wants to study, not play with the suitcase.

20. **When the author says that Christina "headed for the bed like a homing pigeon," she means that Christina —**

    A   flapped her arms

    B   looked like a bird

    C   could not be stopped

    D   made cooing noises

GO ON

A Summer Job

Tom looked out the window. The rain streaming down from the dark sky made it hard to see across the street. He sighed heavily and turned away. He took two steps and flopped down on the couch with a groan. "I hate summer," he announced to no one in particular.

"What's the problem?" his mom asked as she came into the room carrying a stack of magazines.

"There's nothing to do," Tom said sadly, as if the gray, rainy weather reflected how he felt.

"Have you read those library books?" his mom asked brightly. "We checked out quite a few last week."

Tom simply nodded unhappily. "I read every one of them twice. They aren't very interesting the third time around."

"You should have gone with Linda to the animal shelter," his mom said. Tom's sister Linda loved animals and spent every spare hour at the shelter.

"Ugh! Walking dogs in this downpour would be a wet, nasty, smelly job."

"Why don't you call Ted? Maybe he could come over, and you could work on that big puzzle we've been trying to finish," his mom suggested.

Tom rolled over and faced the back of the couch. "He's gone to see his uncle in Ohio."

"Well then," his mom said, "I guess it's up to me to find something for you to do." She put the magazines on the table and walked upstairs. Tom stayed on the couch, staring glumly at nothing in particular.

Within a few minutes she returned. This time she was carrying a pile of thin books. Tom's little brother Joe trailed behind her looking disgusted. Four years younger than Tom, he had just finished first grade.

"Here," Tom's mom handed him the books. "Joe needs to work on his reading this summer, and you're going to help him."

Before Tom could protest, she left the room.

"Not going to do it," Joe muttered angrily. "I hate reading."

Tom opened one of Joe's little books. It was the story of a puppy. The book was simple and dull. As if the day wasn't bad enough, Tom thought, I have to read this!

Joe closed his eyes and refused to even look at the book. "NO!" he said loudly.

Suddenly Tom had an idea. "Listen," he said, "how would you like to have your very own book about something you like? Would you read it?"

Joe opened one eye. "Could it be about chickens?" he asked.

This chicken lives on a farm.

"It can be about whatever you want," Tom said firmly.

With Mom's permission, they cut out pictures from the magazines. Then they glued them to sheets of paper. Joe decided what he wanted each page to say, and Tom carefully wrote the sentences. When they finished, Tom stapled the pages together.

When Linda got home, Joe could hardly wait to read to her from his new book.

"Can we make another book tomorrow even if it's not raining?" Joe asked hopefully.

"We can make as many as you want," Tom told him, smiling.

21. **Why is Tom unhappy when the story begins?**

   A He does not like rainy weather.

   B He has nothing interesting to do.

   C His friend is out of town.

   D His brother is bothering him.

22. **Tom does not want to help Linda because —**

   A the shelter is far away

   B he does not like dogs

   C the job would be unpleasant

   D he does not like Linda

GO ON

23. **At the end of the story, Tom probably feels —**

    A calm

    B lonely

    C pleased

    D nervous

24. **Why does Joe close his eyes?**

    A He does not want to look at his mom.

    B He is tired and wants to sleep.

    C He does not want to read the book.

    D He does not like his brother.

25. **Which word BEST describes Tom?**

    A thankful

    B playful

    C curious

    D clever

26. **How are Joe and Tom ALIKE?**

    A Both like interesting books.

    B Both like to spend time with their sister.

    C Both work on big puzzles.

    D Both enjoy library visits.

27. **What do Tom and Joe do LAST when they are making the book?**

    A cut pictures from magazines

    B staple the pages together

    C glue pictures to the pages

    D wrote sentences on the pages

28. **The author MOST LIKELY believes that —**

    A it is a mistake to tell your mom you have nothing to do

    B everyone should read library books as often as possible

    C when you help someone else, you help yourself as well

    D learning to read can be difficult

29. **Where does this story take place?**

    A in the library

    B at Tom's school

    C in a bookstore

    D at Tom and Joe's houses

GO ON

Soccer: You Can Do It

by Kirk Bizley

One way of getting used to a soccer ball is to practice catching and throwing it. Start by rolling the ball along the ground. Practice with a partner. Roll the ball to each other. Try picking the ball up in two hands as it comes to you.

Goalkeepers are the only players who are allowed to use their hands in a soccer game while the ball is in play. Now try a throw-in. Use two hands. Snap your body forward as you throw the ball from above your head. You can practice throw-ins with a partner. You can even practice goalkeepers' catches when the ball is thrown.

You can make the throws a bit different by throwing down. This makes the ball bounce before it gets to your partner.

Learn to kick the ball correctly so you don't hurt your foot. For short kicks and passes, kick with the inside of your foot. Never kick with your toes!

Begin by putting the ball next to your foot. Make sure the ball is not moving before you kick it. Try kicking the ball with your left foot and your right foot.

For fun, try kicking at targets. Cones make good targets. See if you can hit them with the ball. Have a partner roll the ball to you. Try using your foot to stop the ball. Make sure you are lined up with the ball as it comes to you.

When you can stop the ball, you have learned to trap the ball. Trapping the ball makes the ball easier to kick away.

Passing means kicking the ball to someone else. In a game, you pass the ball to your teammates.

To pass, you need to practice controlling the ball. You need to be able to kick it just where you want. Practice passing with a partner. Start close to each other. Don't move further apart until you can trap and pass the ball every time.

GO ON

30. **Which of these sentences from the passage is an OPINION?**

    A   Start by rolling the ball along the ground.

    B   Practice with a partner.

    C   You can practice throw-ins with a partner.

    D   Cones make good targets.

31. **The author thinks that a good way to control the ball when you kick is to —**

    A   trap the ball

    B   use your toes

    C   throw down the ball

    D   snap your body forward

32. **What is the FIRST thing the author says to do to get used to a soccer ball?**

    A   practice catching and throwing a soccer ball

    B   put the ball by your foot and trap it

    C   kick the soccer ball when it is moving

    D   kick the soccer ball with your right foot

33. **According to the author, why should you learn to kick correctly?**

    A   so you can win the game

    B   so you don't hurt your foot

    C   so you won't miss the ball

    D   so you can throw the ball

34. **What is the BEST summary of the last paragraph?**

    A   Learn to control the ball by passing it to a partner.

    B   Kicking the ball to someone else is a helpful skill.

    C   Pass the ball to a partner when you can.

    D   Kicking at targets is a good way to practice.

35. **Goalkeepers are DIFFERENT from other soccer players because they can —**

    A   use their right foot

    B   pass the ball

    C   kick the ball

    D   use their hands

GO ON

Blowing Bubbles

1 Children may have played with bubbles since soap was invented. Several hundred years ago, they used leftover washing soap. This soap was the only way they had to make bubbles. In 1940 a person in a company that made cleaning supplies had an idea. The company sold bottles of something that looked like water. In fact, the mixture made bubbles. Now this mixture is the best selling toy in the world. Today grown-ups and children alike blow bubbles.

2 Bubbles can be made in many sizes. The small bottles sold at the store make little bubbles. Some bubble experts can make bubbles big enough to hold two people. The people can stand four to eight feet apart. They are still in the middle of a bubble. The longest bubble on record was fifty feet. How do you make these super bubbles?

3 First, make your own bubble liquid. Use dish soap, water, and sugar. Let the mixture sit overnight. Now the fun begins! Almost anything can be used to make bubbles. You can bend a hanger or use a funnel, a straw, or even a string formed into a loop. Get your hands wet with bubble mixture, and you can hold bubbles. Remember, this mixture is very slippery. Be careful not to spill it.

4 A paper cone makes good bubbles. Roll two sheets of paper tightly into a cone. The opening at the large end should be $1\frac{1}{2}$ inches. Tape the cone with masking tape. Put the tape closer to the narrow end. You do not want the tape to get wet. Cut the narrow end of the cone. This will be a mouth piece. It should be small. Then cut the wide end of the cone. Make it as smooth and round as you can. Stand the cone up on this end. If it does not stand up, trim it until it does. You can use this cone many times. Let it dry out after each use.

5 The first time you use it, dip the cone into the mixture for a few seconds. Tap it lightly on the side of the dish to get rid of extra liquid. Then slowly blow your bubble. Hold the cone pointing down at first. Then as the bubble gets bigger, you can lift it up. When you have the size bubble you

GO ON

want, rapidly flip the cone down or up. Your bubble will float away. Bubbles are not very strong. You will make better bubbles on days where there is very little wind.

6 You can play bubble games with your friends. Have a bubble race and see who can keep a bubble in the air longest. See who can guide a bubble to the finish line. You can even freeze a bubble. Wet a plate and blow a bubble onto the plate. Carefully put the plate in a freezer away from the door. In about two minutes, slowly open the door. Your bubble is frozen.

7 Bubbles can be fun for people of all ages!

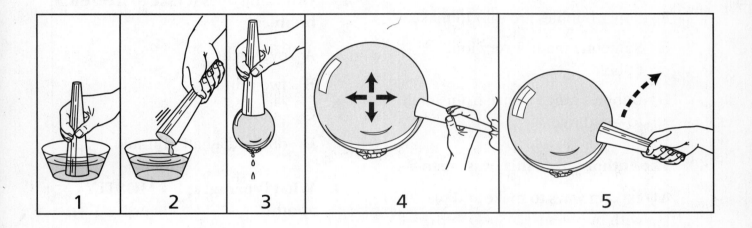

36. **According to the diagram, what is the FIRST step when you make bubbles?**

   A Flip the bubble off the cone.

   B Tap the cone lightly.

   C Dip the cone into the mixture.

   D Slowly blow a bubble.

37. **Which sentence describes what is happening in step 5 of the diagram?**

   A The bubble is getting bigger.

   B The bubble is being blown upward.

   C The bubble is being flipped off the cone.

   D The bubble is being formed.

38. According to the passage, when were bubbles first sold as a toy?

   A 1910

   B 1920

   C 1930

   (D) 1940

39. Which sentence tells the main idea of paragraph 2?

   A A big bubble can hold two people inside.

   B Super bubbles are easy to make.

   C Someone made a very long bubble.

   (D) Bubbles range in size from small to very large.

40. The author wrote this passage to —

   A explain ways to make and play with bubbles

   B persuade people to buy more bubble mixture

   (C) tell stories about different kinds of bubbles

   D explain what a bubble expert does

41. Why should you tape the cone close to the narrow end?

   A so the tape will stick better

   B so the cone will stand up

   (C) so the tape will stay dry

   D so the cone will be smooth

42. Why is it better to make bubbles on days that are not very windy?

   A The bubble mixture will last longer.

   B The wind will make the bubbles get too big.

   C The wind will quickly break the bubbles.

   (D) The bubbles will not float very far.

43. How long does it take to freeze a bubble?

   A overnight

   (B) two minutes

   C one day

   D one and a half minutes

44. What is paragraph 1 MOSTLY about?

   A how to make bubbles with dish soap

   B the history of bubbles

   C how to blow bubbles with a funnel

   (D) the games children play with bubbles

 GO ON

The Paper Crane

by Molly Bang

A man once owned a restaurant on a busy road. He loved to cook good food and he loved to serve it. He worked from morning until night, and he was happy.

But a new highway was built close by. Travelers drove straight from one place to another and no longer stopped at the restaurant. Many days went by when no guests came at all. The man became very poor, and had nothing to do but dust and polish his empty plates and tables.

One evening a stranger came into the restaurant. His clothes were old and worn, but he had an unusual, gentle manner.

Though he said he had no money to pay for food, the owner invited him to sit down. He cooked the best meal he could make and served him like a king. When the stranger had finished, he said to his host, "I cannot pay you with money, but I would like to thank you in my own way."

He picked up a paper napkin from the table and folded it into the shape of a crane. "You have only to clap your hands," he said, "and this bird will come to life and dance for you. Take it, and enjoy it while it is with you." With these words the stranger left.

It happened just as the stranger had said. The owner had only to clap his hands and the paper crane became a living bird, flew down to the floor, and danced.

Soon word of the dancing crane spread, and people came from far and near to see the magic bird perform. The owner was happy again, for his restaurant was always full of guests. He cooked and served and had company from morning until night.

The weeks passed. And the months.

GO ON

One evening a man came into the restaurant. His clothes were old and worn, but he had an unusual, gentle manner. The owner knew him at once and was overjoyed. The stranger, however, said nothing. He took a flute from his pocket, raised it to his lips, and began to play.

The crane flew down from its place on the shelf and danced as it had never danced before.

The stranger finished playing, lowered the flute from his lips, and returned it to his pocket. He climbed on the back of the crane, and they flew out of the door and away.

The restaurant still stands by the side of the road, and guests still come to eat the good food and hear the story of the gentle stranger and the magic crane made from a paper napkin. But neither the stranger nor the dancing crane has ever been seen again.

45. **Where does the story take place?**

    A in an inn

    B in a dream

    C in a restaurant

    D in a house

46. **What is the MAIN message of the story?**

    A Paper can be magical.

    B Kindness is often rewarded.

    C People like unusual things.

    D Bad luck cannot be avoided.

47. **What happens when the stranger returns to the restaurant?**

    A He plays a flute.

    B He eats a large meal.

    C He pays for his food.

    D He dances with the crane.

48. **How is the stranger different on his second visit?**

    A He has on a shabby hat.

    B He wears different clothes.

    C He does not speak.

    D He smiles a lot.

GO ON

Origami

1   Have you ever made a paper airplane? If so, you are doing some basic paper folding. Over the years, people have turned this simple work into an art form. It is called origami. It was developed in Asia long ago. Origami means "folding paper" in Japanese.

2   Paper was first developed in China in A.D. 105. People in Japan learned about paper in the early seventh century. They developed a special kind of paper. It was strong, yet soft, and did not tear easily. This is the paper they used for origami. They began folding paper about 1,200 years ago.

3   At first, folded paper was used as a kind of gift wrap for food. Later, people made different animals. Beginning about 1600, special "bases" were made. These are starting folds. They were used to make birds and frogs. From about 1688 to 1704, people even used paper cranes and boats as designs on their clothes. Legend says that if someone folds 1,000 cranes, he or she will have good luck. Many people began folding paper. The designs were passed down from mother to daughter. Nothing was written down at first. As time went on, new designs were developed. Many were very hard to make.

4   Anyone can make an easy origami design. You can use plain writing paper. You can even use dollar bills or business cards. The easiest designs begin with a square piece of paper. It is helpful to work on a smooth, hard surface. A table top or desk is a good place to start. A hard surface means that your folds can be made carefully. The best way to learn is to practice folding. Different designs and directions can be found on the Internet. You must follow each step carefully. Do not skip a step. Most people do not like to cut or glue the paper. They use one sheet for each design.

5   Today, paper folding is done in nearly every country. You can find examples in pop-up books, cards, and crafts. A new approach is to use printed cloth instead of paper. Owls, frogs, boxes, even small purses can be made. Whether you are folding paper or cloth, you can make many different objects. Imagine making a pecking bird or a frog on a lily pad out of paper! Do you think you could fold 1,000 cranes?

GO ON

49. **Which of these statements from the passage is an OPINION?**

   A Paper was first developed in China in A.D. 105.

   B Later, people made different animals.

   C Nothing was written down at first.

   D Many were very hard to make.

50. **Paper made in Japan was ideal for origami because it was —**

   A strong and soft

   B black and white

   C small and round

   D used for food

51. **What is the BEST summary of paragraph 4?**

   A Origami is easy if you follow the steps.

   B Paper must be folded on a hard surface.

   C Many people use glue and scissors.

   D Origami needs several sheets of paper.

52. **When did people in Japan first start folding paper?**

   A before A.D. 105

   B 1,200 years ago

   C around A.D. 1600

   D in modern times

53. **Why did the author write this passage?**

   A to tell a story about origami

   B to persuade people to learn origami

   C to give some information about origami

   D to explain why people like origami

Use "Origami" and "The Paper Crane" to answer questions 54 and 55.

54. **The essay and the story both tell about —**

   A a magical paper crane

   B unusual paper animals

   C people from Asia

   D different ways to fold paper

55. **The stranger probably made a crane instead of a frog because —**

   A cranes were thought to be lucky

   B cranes were easier to make

   C people would not like a frog

   D he could fold only one design

(GO ON

Mai is in fourth grade. She wrote this report about her summer for English class. She wants you to help her revise and edit the report. Read it and think about the changes she should make.

A Great Summer Day

(1) This summer we had a fun event in our neighborhood called "Night Out." (2) A big red, white, and blue banner was strung across the street. (3) It said: "United We Stand!" and meant that everybody should stick together and help each other out.

(4) Everyone in our neighborhood got together and brought food. (5) The streets were blocked off, and we brought our lawn chairs to sit on. (6) I do not like those green lawn chairs. (7) We had tacos, beans fresh carrots from the community garden, and sandwiches.

(8) I met Ryan, who just moved into one of the apartment buildings on our street. (9) I found out that he would be going to my school and would be in the same grade.

(10) People from the centerville police and fire departments were there and handed out safety information. (11) The power company handed out some knew pencils, and we got free cardboard fans from the water company, too. (12) We played games like ring toss and basketball free throws. (13) We each won a little prize even if we didn't win the game. (14) That was the best night of the whole summer!

GO ON

56. Which sentence could BEST be added before sentence 8?

  A Mrs. Alvarez made a huge chocolate cake for dessert.

  B I thought the banner should be left up all year.

  C The games that we got to play were a lot of fun.

  D We talked to our neighbors and got to know new people.

57. Which sentence does NOT belong in the report?

  A sentence 2

  B sentence 6

  C sentence 10

  D sentence 12

58. The purpose of this report is to —

  A persuade readers to join a special event

  B tell about something that happened

  C explain how to have a "Night Out"

  D entertain readers with a funny story

59. What change should be made to sentence 7?

  A change had to has

  B add a comma after beans

  C change sandwiches to sandwichs

  D make no change

60. What change should be made to sentence 11?

  A change knew to new

  B change pencils to penciles

  C change too to two

  D make no change

61. Which word from sentence 13 is a noun?

  A little

  B prize

  C we

  D won

62. What change should be made to sentence 10?

  A change there to they're

  B change safety to safty

  C change centerville to Centerville

  D make no change

GO ON

Gilbert is in fourth grade. He wrote this essay about fourth grade at the end of the school year. He wants you to help him revise and edit the essay. Read it and think about the changes he should make.

The Best Year Ever

(1) Fourth grade were the most fun in school so far. (2) I learned about fractions and measuring in math and I made paper masks for art. (3) I read about the American colonys and wrote about them.

(4) Best of all, the class had special study units. (5) For example, each of us had to study a state and learn all about it. (6) I studied Texas because that's where my cousins live. (7) I made a map of texas and drew a picture of the Alamo and some oil wells.

(8) I also liked the games we played, such as volleyball and soccer. (9) Our volleyball team did not win many games, but we had a lot of fun.

(10) The greatest thing about fourth grade was our teacher, Mr. Swinnon. (11) He showed us science experiments. (12) We always liked that because Mr. Swinnon sometimes had a hard time making an experiment come out the way it should. (13) He laughed the loudest when that happened.

(14) I hope fifth grade at lincoln School will be as much fun.

63. **What change should be made to sentence 3?**

   A change American to american

   B change colonys to colonies

   C change them to it

   D make no change

64. Which sentence could BEST be added after sentence 9?

   A After school some of us play softball in my yard.

   B Our coach always tells us the rules of each game.

   C Playing different games is a lot of fun, but I really like to play baseball.

   D Our soccer team had a great year, though, and almost won the championship.

65. Which sentence could BEST be added after sentence 14?

   A I really like school, but I think those reports are hard to write.

   B I have a friend who is in fifth grade now.

   C Fourth grade was a great year, and I'm sorry to see it end.

   D Mr. Swinnon does not teach fifth grade.

66. What change should be made to sentence 6?

   A change <u>studyed</u> to <u>studied</u>

   B change <u>that's</u> to <u>thats</u>

   C change <u>where</u> to <u>wear</u>

   D make no change

67. What change should be made to sentence 2?

   A change <u>learned</u> to <u>lerned</u>

   B add a comma after <u>math</u>

   C change the period to a question mark

   D make no change

68. Which word from sentence 12 is a pronoun?

   A liked

   B because

   C an

   D it

69. What change should be made to sentence 1?

   A change <u>Fourth</u> to <u>fourth</u>

   B change <u>were</u> to <u>was</u>

   C change <u>school</u> to <u>School</u>

   D make no change

70. What change should be made to sentence 14?

   A change <u>fifth</u> to <u>Fifth</u>

   B change <u>lincoln</u> to <u>Lincoln</u>

   C change <u>hope</u> to <u>hopes</u>

   D make no change

GO ON

Allison is in fourth grade. She wrote this report about the state of Illinois. She wants you to help her revise and edit the report. Read it and think about the changes she should make.

The State of Illinois

(1) I chose Illinois as my state because I like reading about Abraham Lincoln. (2) He lived in Illinois, and so did President Ronald Reagan.

(3) Chicago is the largest city, and it is home to the first big aquarium that opened in 1893. (4) Chicago is located on Lake Michigan, the only one of the Great Lakes that is totally inside the United States. (5) The first skyscraper in the world was built in Chicago in 1885. (6) Chicago is called the "Windy City" and has the largest public library in the world.

(7) Two important zoos in Illinois is the Lincoln Park Zoo and the Brookfield Zoo. (8) The first animal in the Lincoln Park Zoo was a bear.

(9) Illinois is famous because barbed wire, the round silo for storing grain, and the tasty ice-cream sundae were invented there.

(10) The state bird is the cardinal, and the state flower is the purple violet. (11) The biggest crop is corn. (12) The most interesting thing I learned about Illinois is that it is home to the largest cookie and cracker factory in the world.

71. What change should be made to sentence 7?

A change Two to Too

B change zoos to zooes

C change is to are

D make no change

72. What is the purpose of this report?

A to inform readers about the state of Illinois

B to persuade people to visit Illinois

C to tell a story about the Lincoln Park Zoo

D to tell about the history of Chicago

Practice Test B

Here are a few tips to keep in mind when you take a test:

- Read all directions and test items carefully.
- Read each answer choice carefully.
- Choose the best answer.

Complete this sample to help you get ready to take this practice test.

SAMPLE

DIRECTIONS: Read the item. Circle the letter of the correct answer.

> **Vincent got a running start before he <u>bounded</u> across the puddle.**

What does the word <u>bounded</u> mean in this sentence?

A   strolled

B   swam

C   jumped

D   crawled

The correct answer is **C**. The word <u>bounded</u> means "jumped." Circle the letter **C**.

Some parts of this test will have passages for you to read. Read each passage carefully. Then answer the questions about the passage.

DIRECTIONS: Read each item. Circle the letter of the correct answer on your *Achieve It!* **Practice Test Answer Sheet.**

1. | She did not smile when I gave her the book, so I thought she was <u>ungrateful</u>.

   If <u>grateful</u> means "thankful," what does <u>ungrateful</u> mean?

   A   thankful after

   B   not thankful

   C   less thankful

   D   thankful about

2. | The frightened deer quickly <u>vanished</u> into the forest.

   Which word means the SAME as <u>vanished</u>?

   A   fell

   B   crawled

   C   disappeared

   D   arrived

3. | When the woman saw the mouse, she was frightened and <u>shrieked</u> loudly.

   Which word means the OPPOSITE of <u>shrieked</u>?

   A   grunted

   B   whispered

   C   screamed

   D   growled

4. | The print in that book is so small that it is <u>difficult</u> to read.

   What word means the OPPOSITE of <u>difficult</u>?

   A   mean

   B   easy

   C   costly

   D   mysterious

5. | When the actors practiced, we got to <u>preview</u> the play.

   If <u>view</u> means "to look at," what does <u>preview</u> mean?

   A   view later

   B   view before

   C   view again

   D   view across

GO ON

6. We watched the woman <u>cast</u> her fishing net into the water.

cast (käst) *n.* **1** the actors in a play **2** a hard plaster covering on a broken arm or leg *v.* **3** to vote **4** to throw

Which meaning BEST fits the way <u>cast</u> is used in this sentence?

A meaning 1

B meaning 2

C meaning 3

D meaning 4

7. The food had a very <u>peculiar</u> smell, so we decided not to eat it.

What does the word <u>peculiar</u> mean in this sentence?

A strange

B amazing

C special

D interesting

8. The speaker was very <u>solemn</u> as he read the sad poem.

What does the word <u>solemn</u> mean in this sentence?

A eager

B astonished

C serious

D tired

9. The cat moved slowly and <u>cautiously</u> as she neared the dog because she didn't want it to chase her.

What does the word <u>cautiously</u> mean in this sentence?

A carefully

B dangerously

C foolishly

D curiously

10. The <u>beam</u> of the car headlights startled the cat sitting in the driveway.

beam (beem) *n.* **1** a long, thick piece of wood or metal used to support a building **2** a ray of light *v.* **3** to have a big smile **4** to shine brightly

Which meaning BEST fits the way <u>beam</u> is used in this sentence?

A meaning 1

B meaning 2

C meaning 3

D meaning 4

GO ON

Jean [John] James Audubon moved to the United States from France in 1803. He became the most famous wildlife artist of his day. Even now, bird artists measure their work against his. This passage is historical fiction about Audubon's childhood.

Audubon: The Man Who Painted Birds

by Norah Smaridge

Jean grew into a handsome and clever boy. By the time he was fourteen, he could play the violin and the flute. But he did not work hard at his lessons. He wanted only to draw birds.

He was happiest in summer. Then Madame took them all to La Gerbetière, a country house not far from Nantes. There were woods and fields all around it. Every day Jean took pad and pencil and hunted for little creatures to draw. He drew a nest of field mice. He drew a woodchuck.

Mostly he drew birds—a coot, a magpie, and a green woodpecker.

When Captain Audubon came home, Jean had hundreds of pictures to show him. "But they are all bad, Papa," he said. "Very, very *bad*. The claws and bills are wrong. And the tails look as if they would fall off!"

"It is not easy to draw something which is alive," said Captain Audubon. He put the drawings aside. "Now show me your lesson books."

Jean went red with shame. His arithmetic and history were very poor. His geography was not much better.

Captain Audubon frowned. "This will not do, Jean," he said. "It is high time you went to school. When I leave, I will take you to Rochefort with me. I will put you in the naval academy there."

A few weeks later, Jean left with his father. "Don't let them be too hard on him," Madame begged her husband. "I hear it is a very strict school."

In four days they were at Rochefort, a town on a rocky hillside. Captain Audubon showed Jean the seawall, the docks, and the battleships. There were officers and sailors everywhere.

Jean started school, and it was even worse than he feared. The rooms were as bare as a prison. The lessons were hard and long, and there were no drawing lessons at all. When Jean saw a sea gull through the window, he thought, "I wish I could fly like that. I would escape!"

He could not fly, but he could jump. One day he jumped out of a window and began to run, but he did not get far. A sailor spotted him and brought him back. Captain Audubon was sent for, and Jean was scared. But the Captain did not scold him. "Maman is right. You are not meant to be a seaman," he said. "But if you want to spend your life drawing, you must learn to do it properly. I shall take you to Paris, to the best teacher in France. His name is Jacques Louis David, and he is a famous artist."

Once again Jean and his father set out on a journey, this time to Paris. They came to a tall house and climbed up to a studio under the roof.

Jean looked around the big studio in surprise. There were no paintings, no drawings. Only great statues of men and women. They were cold and white, with empty eyes.

A man in a smock came to greet them. "So this is young Jean Audubon, who wants to learn to draw," he said.

"Will you teach me to draw birds properly, sir?" Jean asked. "I want them to be alive. I want them to fly on the paper! I want—"

"You are in too much of a hurry, young man!" David said, laughing. "First you must learn to draw these plaster casts. This—and this—and this." He pointed to the great white statues.

Jean's heart sank. He wanted to beg his father to take him home, but he did not dare.

He was not happy in David's studio. He wanted to draw tiny creatures but the painter would not let him. He made Jean copy all the big white casts in the studio. Day after day passed, and Jean was not allowed to draw a bird.

Jean hated the studio. He did not like to draw men and women with dead eyes. He often left his work and went to look out of the window. He longed to draw the sparrows in the street. They were so alive. They moved so quickly.

One day he packed his bag and climbed into a coach for home. As it bowled along, he began to feel happy. When it reached Nantes, he jumped out and ran all the way to the house. "Maman!" he shouted. "It is I, Jean. I am home for good!"

Madame Audubon came running. So did Rosa. Captain Audubon followed them, looking grave. "I am sorry, Papa, but I cannot work with David," Jean said. "I cannot paint plaster casts. I want to paint living things. Please let me stay home!"

Captain Audubon looked at his wife. "Oh, please!" she said. He nodded. "Very well, you may stay home and study—until I can think of a plan for you," he said.

Jean was happy again. All day long he sat on the riverbank, reading and drawing. Slowly, the birds began to look right. Their little claws seemed to clutch at the branches. Their tails looked real.

11. **Why does Jean run away from the naval academy?**

   A There are no drawing lessons.

   B He fails his classes.

   C He gets in trouble for drawing.

   D His mother is sick and needs him.

12. **What does Captain Audubon do when Jean returns home from David's studio?**

   A He punishes Jean.

   B He allows Jean to study at home.

   C He forces Jean to return to the studio.

   D He apologizes to David.

13. **Jean dislikes David's studio because it is —**

   A cold and dark

   B dirty and smells bad

   C filled with lifeless statues

   D located far from where Jean lives

14. **What event happens FIRST in the story?**

   A Jean goes to Paris to study drawing.

   B Jean goes to the naval academy.

   C Jean learns to draw birds very well.

   D Jean does poorly in his school lessons.

GO ON

15. **What can you tell about Maman from reading the story?**

    A   She wants Jean to be a seaman.

    B   She understands how Jean feels.

    C   She wants to help Jean run away.

    D   She worries that Jean will learn to draw.

16. **Jean goes to the naval academy because —**

    A   his father wants him to learn how to draw boats

    B   his father wants him to stop running away

    C   he wants to be a sailor

    D   he is not doing well with his lessons

17. **How are David's studio and the naval academy ALIKE?**

    A   The work is dull and not what Jean wants to do.

    B   The walls are filled with drawings of birds.

    C   Jean's teachers are bad tempered.

    D   There are statues that are difficult to draw.

18. **Where is Jean happiest during his childhood?**

    A   in David's studio

    B   at the family's country home

    C   at the naval academy

    D   on the seawall and the docks

19. **Which word BEST describes Jean at the end of the story?**

    A   lively

    B   careless

    C   happy

    D   amused

20. **The author wrote this story to —**

    A   entertain readers with a story about an artist

    B   give information about a famous art school

    C   persuade readers to study wildlife drawings

    D   explain how to draw animals that look real

21. **What is the MAIN problem in the story?**

    A   Jean likes his classes but not his teachers.

    B   Jean's father is angry with him about his poor lessons.

    C   Jean and his father do not agree about plans for Jean's education.

    D   Jean loves to play music, but his father wants him to be a sailor.

GO ON

The Candlewick Book of Fairy Tales: Rapunzel

Retold by Sarah Hayes

There was once a poor peasant who lived next door to a witch. He and his wife longed for a child, and eventually their wish was granted. As the day drew near for the baby to be born, the peasant's wife began to spend all her time gazing at the vegetables in the witch's garden. At last she could stand it no longer.

"Husband!" she cried. "You must fetch me some of the rampion that grows in the witch's garden, or I shall die." The peasant looked at his wife and saw how pale she had become, and he knew she spoke the truth. When it was dark, he climbed over the high wall and dropped into the witch's garden. He quickly dug up a few rampion roots, which he took back for his wife. She ate the rampion greedily, and by morning she was asking for more. This time the witch was waiting in her garden when the peasant climbed over the wall.

"He who steals my rampion will pay for it with his life!" shrieked the witch.

"It is f-for my w-wife," stammered the peasant. "She will die without it, and the baby too."

The witch thought for a moment. "Give me your baby and I shall spare your life." The peasant was so terrified that he agreed, and as soon as the baby was born, the witch came and took it away. She called the baby Rapunzel after the rampion the peasant had stolen from her garden.

Rapunzel grew up to be a beautiful girl with very long golden hair. On the day of her twelfth birthday, she was taken into the forest by the witch and shut up in a high tower that had neither a door nor stairs. Whenever the witch wanted to go to Rapunzel's room, she stood at the foot of the

GO ON

tower and said, "Rapunzel, Rapunzel, let down your hair." Then Rapunzel let her hair hang down from the window, and the witch grabbed hold of it and clambered up the wall.

Rapunzel was often lonely in her room, and sometimes she would gaze out across the forest and sing sad songs. One day a king's son was out hunting when he heard the beautiful sad singing and rode toward it. He looked up at the tower, but he could not see Rapunzel's face, for the window was too high. He searched in vain for a door or a stairway and vowed he would return the following day.

True to his word, he came the next day, and the next. On the third day the king's son saw the witch arrive at the tower, and he quickly hid behind a tree. He heard the witch call for Rapunzel, and watched the golden hair come tumbling down and the witch go climbing up. He waited until the witch had gone, and then he came to the foot of the tower.

"Rapunzel, Rapunzel, let down your hair!" he cried, and the golden hair came tumbling down. In a moment he had climbed up the tower and entered Rapunzel's room.

Rapunzel was very frightened at first, for she had never seen a man before. But the king's son visited her every day, and soon she fell in love with him. Every time he came, the king's son brought a skein of silk. And while the witch was away, Rapunzel sewed the silk to make a ladder so that she could escape from the tower and marry the king's son. Soon the ladder was nearly finished, and Rapunzel could think of nothing but her escape. One day she said to the witch without thinking, "Why is it that you take so long to climb the tower? The king's son is with me in an instant."

Then the witch knew that the king's son had been to visit Rapunzel, and she was furious. She took a pair of scissors and cut off all Rapunzel's golden hair.

Then she sent her away to wander in the desert. She fastened the hair to the windowsill and sat down to wait. Toward evening the king's son arrived and cried out, "Rapunzel, Rapunzel, let down your hair!" The witch threw the golden hair out of the window and in an instant the king's son was up

GO ON

the tower. When he reached the window, there, to his horror, was the witch, who shrieked out, "Your singing bird has flown the nest. Cat got her first; your eyes are next!"

The king's son was so overcome with grief that he threw himself out of the window. He fell onto a thornbush, which scratched his eyes and blinded him. For a year he wandered sorrowfully about the world until one day he came to a desert and heard the sweet sad voice of Rapunzel, whom he thought was dead. When she saw his poor blind eyes, Rapunzel began to weep. And as her tears fell on his eyes, the king's son began to see again.

Rapunzel and he were soon married, and they lived happily ever after.

[Rampion is a vegetable grown in Europe. It is rather like a radish, but the roots taste sweeter. The roots are either boiled or eaten raw.]

22. How does the witch get up to the tower?

A She asks Rapunzel to open the door.

B She flies up on a broom.

C She climbs up on a ladder.

D She uses Rapunzel's hair as a rope.

23. What happens AFTER Rapunzel turns twelve?

A She is taken into the forest.

B She returns to her parents.

C She lives with the witch.

D She suddenly becomes pretty.

24. This story was written to —

A entertain readers with a make-believe story

B persuade readers to eat rampion

C warn readers about witches

D inform readers about eating vegetables

25. Why does the king's son bring Rapunzel a skein of silk?

A to make pretty hair ribbons

B to weave into a lovely dress

C to knit into a warm blanket

D to sew a ladder to escape

GO ON

26. **Why does the witch send Rapunzel to the desert?**

    A   to keep her away from the prince

    B   to give her a better place to live

    C   to let the people hear her sing

    D   to set her free from the tower

27. **Why does the peasant agree to give up his child?**

    A   He wants to save his wife's life.

    B   He hopes the witch will like him.

    C   He fears the witch will kill him.

    D   He wants her to become a princess.

28. **Why did the witch cut off Rapunzel's hair?**

    A   to weave it into a wig

    B   to trick the prince

    C   to bring it to Rapunzel's father

    D   to make Rapunzel ugly

29. **This story takes place —**

    A   in a large city

    B   on a dairy farm

    C   on a desert island

    D   in a make-believe kingdom

30. **The tower stands for Rapunzel's —**

    A   anger

    B   fear

    C   loneliness

    D   joy

31. **Rapunzel is a singing bird that has flown the nest.**

    This sentence is an example of —

    A   simile

    B   metaphor

    C   alliteration

    D   hyperbole

GO ON

Japan

by David F. Marx

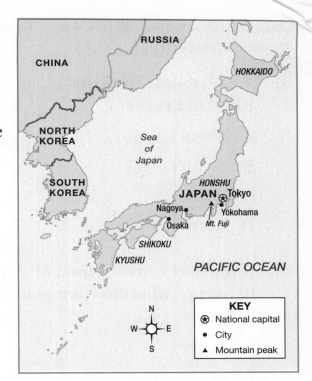

1 Japan is a country in Asia. It is made up of many islands, large and small. People who live in Japan are called "Japanese." That is also the name of the language spoken in Japan.

2 Japan has four large islands where most people live. Their names are Hokkaido, Honshu, Shikoku, and Kyushu. Not many people live on the hundreds of smaller islands that are also part of Japan. Some are too tiny to build a house on!

3 Japan is surrounded by water. To the west is the Sea of Japan. To the east is the big Pacific Ocean. If you sail east across the Pacific Ocean, you'll reach California in the United States. To the west, across the Sea of Japan, are Japan's neighbor countries: South Korea, North Korea, China, and Russia.

4 Tokyo, the capital of Japan, is on the island of Honshu. It is home to more than eight million people. Tokyo is an exciting, crowded city. From Tokyo, you can see the Pacific Ocean to the east and Mount Fuji to the west. Mount Fuji is the tallest of Japan's many mountains. Its peak, or top, is 12,338 feet above the sea.

5 Most of Japan's 123 million people live in Tokyo and other big cities. These include Yokohama, Osaka, and Nagoya. Many people who live in these cities work in businesses such as stores, banks, and factories. Cars, computers, and televisions made in Japan are used by people all over the world.

6 Japanese people earn a living in other ways, too. Living on the seacoast, many people catch and sell fish and seaweed. These are important foods in Japan. Living along rivers, farmers grow rice in soggy rice paddies. In Japan, rice is eaten with almost every meal. Living near mountains, some people work in mines. These people dig useful rocks out of the ground. Japanese people have learned to live in a place where the land meets the water, and where the mountains reach to the sky.

GO ON

Look at the map of Japan. Use it to answer questions 32 and 33.

32. **Which country is closest to the island of Kyushu?**

   A   North Korea

   B   South Korea

   C   China

   D   Russia

33. **If you were traveling from Mt. Fuji to Nagoya, what direction would you travel?**

   A   north

   B   south

   C   east

   D   west

34. **Which of these sentences from the passage is an OPINION?**

   A   To the east is the big Pacific Ocean.

   B   Tokyo, the capital of Japan, is on the island of Honshu.

   C   Tokyo is an exciting, crowded city.

   D   Japanese people earn a living in other ways, too.

35. **Which foods are eaten the most in Japan?**

   A   meat and cheese

   B   vegetables and fruits

   C   fish and rice

   D   beans and corn

36. **What is the main idea of paragraph 5?**

   A   Most Japanese live and work in large cities.

   B   Japan has a population of 123 million people.

   C   The largest cities in Japan are Tokyo and Yokohama.

   D   People who live in big cities have many different jobs.

37. **What is the BEST summary of the passage?**

   A   Many people live in Japan, a group of islands located near China, North Korea, South Korea, and Russia. Japan has mountains.

   B   Japan has many people. The capital of Japan is Tokyo, and 8 million people live there.

   C   Many people in Japan work in factories or catch and sell fish. Other people live on islands.

   D   Japan is an Asian country made up of four islands. Most people live and work in the big cities, but some earn a living in other ways.

GO ON

The Big Play

"I am so sick of that play I could scream!" Josie said through gritted teeth.

Leon nodded in agreement. "I know the part better than she does." They were talking about their friend Sarah.

"All we do now is help Sarah practice," Rob complained.

The three friends were sitting in the school lunch room waiting for Sarah. She had asked them to come to play practice.

"There you guys are!" Sarah said as she dashed in. "Well, come on!" She turned and hurried out without waiting for a reply.

The three friends stood slowly and trudged into the school auditorium. They took seats in the back. As the actors started saying their lines, Rob, Josie, and Leon mouthed the words along with them.

"Marie," Clint said to Sarah, "there's a big storm brewing. It looks bad!"

"Oh, dear," Sarah answered, using her most frightened voice, "listen to the wind!"

Suddenly a man shouted, "STOP! This is TERRIBLE!!!" Mr. Biggs, the director, stomped onto the stage.

Sarah looked as if she were going to burst into tears. "What's wrong?" she asked in a trembling voice.

"Do you hear a storm?" he yelled. "Does it sound like rain and thunder? NO, it does not! I have no idea why I agreed to direct this mess."

"Mr. Biggs?" Clint raised his hand as if he were in class. "You can get different sounds from the Internet. Then we can play them, and it will sound stormy."

"HOW are we going to play them?" Mr. Biggs demanded angrily. "We don't have the money for that fancy equipment. I should never have agreed to direct this play. I quit! I will not do this because it can't be done." He turned to walk off the stage, and Sarah did, in fact, start to cry.

"Wait a minute!" Josie leaped from her seat and ran down the aisle. "Mr. Biggs, wait a minute. Can you put a microphone backstage?"

The director stopped and looked at Josie. "I suppose so. Why?"

"Please, keep practicing now. And give me until tomorrow. Have that mike backstage for me then."

Mr. Biggs looked at her suspiciously. "What are you up to, young lady?" His words were nearly drowned out by the actors, pleading with him to continue. "All right! All right! We will continue today, but just for today."

GO ON

Josie hurried back up the aisle and motioned for her friends to follow. Once outside the auditorium, she explained her plan.

The next day, after school, Josie's grandpa arrived at the auditorium carrying a big box. The three friends were waiting for him.

"Josie," Grandpa said, "fill this watering can with water. You boys help me unpack this stuff. Where's the microphone?"

In a few minutes they had everything set up.

"Well?" Mr. Biggs's voice boomed from the front of the curtains. "Are we having a play or are we not?"

"We are, sir," Josie said into the microphone. "Start the action."

Just as Clint said his lines, Rob blew gently into the microphone. The sound of wind filled the stage. After Sarah's line, Leon hit a tin cookie sheet with a spoon and shook it while Josie poured water from the watering can onto another cookie sheet. Thunder and rain echoed across the stage.

Quickly Rob picked up a piece of wood and, holding it by the microphone, knocked on it twice. Right on cue, Sarah said her next line, "There's someone at the door! Quick! Come in!" Josh walked on stage and began his lines.

"STOP!" Mr. Biggs shouted. "Everybody on stage, including the people by the mike."

With long faces, fearing the worst, the actors, Josie, Rob, and Leon came on stage, and so did Josie's grandpa.

When Mr. Biggs saw him, he started to grin. "Ed, I might have known this was your work." Mr. Biggs explained that he and Josie's grandpa had acted in the town's Little Theater group for several years. "So how did you get roped into this?" he asked Josie's grandpa.

"I used to work in radio, remember? I'm just helping the kids get started with the sounds. Then they're on their own."

"They'll need to practice some more before opening night," Mr. Biggs said. "The play must go on!"

The actors cheered and Sarah gave Josie, Rob, and Leon big hugs.

The night of the play, the three friends stood expectantly backstage waiting for the curtain to go up. As Sarah said her lines, they made the sound of rain and thunder. She paused, waiting for the sound of knocking. As Rob reached for the piece of wood, he stopped. Josh was not waiting behind the door. He was late! Quickly Rob blew more heavily into the

GO ON

microphone. Leon bashed the cookie tray harder. Josie poured more water onto the cookie sheet. They could not see what was happening onstage. Then they heard Sarah making up lines. "It sounds like it might be a tornado, Frank! The storm is getting worse! My garden will be washed away!" At that moment, Josh scooted to the set door. Rob grabbed the wood and knocked. "Quick! Come in!" Sarah said, her voice full of relief.

The rest of the play went smoothly. As the curtain went down, Sarah dashed back to her friends. "Come on," she insisted, "you're taking the curtain call with me. You saved the play TWICE!"

38. **Which word BEST describes Josie?**

A grateful

B playful

C curious

D clever

39. **What is one lesson the characters learn in this story?**

A It is good to take one step at a time.

B Friends can work together to solve a problem.

C It is important to be the best actor.

D People should learn to act in plays.

40. **What is another lesson the characters learn in this story?**

A Sound effects can ruin a play.

B An older person's experience can be helpful.

C Radio is better than the Internet.

D It is difficult to be the director of a play.

41. **Which of these could BEST be added at the end of the last paragraph?**

A Josie decided to try out for the next play to see if she could get a starring role.

B Mr. Biggs was pleased because the play went very well.

C Sarah led her friends onstage, and they bowed as the crowd clapped loudly.

D The friends worked hard learning to make new sounds.

GO ON

42. **Why is Mr. Biggs so angry at the beginning of the story?**

   A He thinks the play will be bad.

   B He wishes he had better actors.

   C He is tired of directing the play.

   D He wants more time to practice.

43. **Why is it helpful that Josie, Leon, and Rob know all the play's lines?**

   A They help Sarah learn her lines.

   B They might want to be in the play.

   C They can take the place of any actor who is sick.

   D They know when to make all the different sounds.

44. **MOST of the action in the story takes place in —**

   A a classroom

   B a school auditorium

   C a house

   D a lunch room

45. **What happens AFTER Mr. Biggs stops the play for the second time?**

   A He recognizes Josie's grandpa.

   B He refuses to direct the play.

   C Josie fills a watering can with water.

   D Josie asks him to keep practicing.

46. **How are Sarah and Josie ALIKE?**

   A Both girls think quickly to solve a problem.

   B Both girls get angry very quickly.

   C Both girls are very impatient.

   D Both girls want to be popular.

GO ON

Sound Effects

1 Would you like to hear a train whistle? The wind whistling in the trees? Almost any sound can be found on the Internet. But sounds were not found there first. Sound effects began on the radio. At first, in the 1920s, radio programs did not need special sounds. Air time was filled with music. Sometimes there were speeches. By the 1930s, people were listening to "soap operas." These stories were on the radio every week. There were many other drama shows as well. All these stories needed special sounds.

2 At first, people who made the sounds were not very good. Often, programs used just music. Usually someone played an organ. That was the least expensive way to get music. Many kids' adventure shows used organ music to show changes of scene or mood. Organists were not given sheet music. They had a sheet of paper with words like "danger" or "countryside" written on it. They made up music that went with the action. Making up music was a difficult task. The shows needed other sounds, too. Sounds helped move the story along. If a person walked down a path to get somewhere, listeners wanted to hear footsteps. These had to seem real.

3 Some sounds were recorded. These were sounds that were too large to bring into a radio station. Car engines or the "walla-walla" sounds of large crowds were recorded. Other sounds, such as those made by animals, were also recorded. It would be hard to get a cricket to chirp exactly when needed.

4 Many simple sounds were made during the program. People used ordinary objects to make the sounds. Any water noise was made with a bucket and some water. Twisting cellophane made the sound of a crackling fire. To make footsteps in snow, someone squeezed a box of corn starch. The sound of a pen on paper was made by scratching sandpaper with a paper clip. Thunder was made by shaking a metal sheet. Two coconut shell halves hit

GO ON

together made the sound of horses' hooves. The sound of wind was made by blowing into a glass jar or simply by blowing softly into a microphone.

5 Many radio stations had a "crash box." This was used to make sounds like breaking dishes. A metal can filled with nails, broken coffee cups, pennies, and gravel can make any sort of crashing noise. A "gravel box" was made of wood and filled with a layer of garden gravel. Blocks of wood "walked" across the gravel to make the sound of boots.

6 Sounds were important to radio stories. They made the stories seem more real. Sound effects make the difference between a good show and a great show.

47. **Which of these sentences BEST summarizes paragraph 3?**

   A The sound of a car engine could not be made easily.

   B Sometimes a cricket chirp or animal sound was recorded.

   C Some sounds were made during the program.

   D Sounds that were difficult to make were often recorded.

48. **According to the article, which of these would you MOST LIKELY hear on radio in the 1920s?**

   A a drama

   B an adventure show

   C music

   D a "soap opera"

49. **What is the main idea of paragraph 4?**

   A Many sounds were made with simple objects.

   B Anyone can make a water noise with a bucket and some water.

   C The sound of a crackling fire can be made with cellophane.

   D Radio programs had many different sounds.

50. **Which of these sentences is an OPINION?**

   A People used ordinary objects to make the sounds.

   B The sound of a pen on paper was made by scratching sandpaper with a paper clip.

   C Thunder was made by shaking a metal sheet.

   D Sound effects make the difference between a good show and a great show.

GO ON